Training the Three-Day Event Horse and Rider

Training the Three-Day Event Horse and Rider

JAMES C. WOFFORD

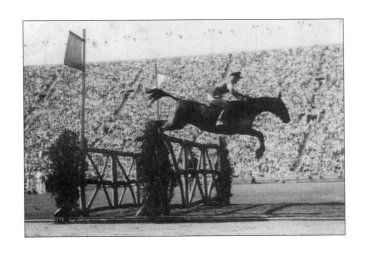

DOUBLEDAY

New York   London   Toronto   Sydney   Auckland

PUBLISHED BY DOUBLEDAY

a division of Bantam Doubleday Dell Publishing Group, Inc.
1540 Broadway, New York, New York 10036

DOUBLEDAY and the portrayal of an anchor with a dolphin are trademarks of Doubleday, a
division of Bantam Doubleday Dell Publishing Group, Inc.

Library of Congress Cataloging-in-Publication Data
Wofford, James C., 1944–
Training the three-day event horse and rider /
James C. Wofford.—1st ed.
p.   cm.
Includes index.
1. Three-day event (Horsemanship)   2. Competition horses—
Training.   3. Horsemen and horsewomen—Training of.   I. Title.
SF295.7.W64   1995
798.2′4—dc20   94-32577
CIP
ISBN 0-385-42520-1

*This book is dedicated with love
to my wife, Gail W. Wofford, M.F.H.,
who stood by me while I learned all that is in
this book, and more.*

Contents

..

Foreword

THE first questions to be asked about any new instructional book are, "Who is the author; does he know what he's talking about; and does his track record justify taking seriously what he has to say?"

With respect to the present book, you might suspect that my long friendship with Jimmy Wofford could prejudice my answers to these very pertinent questions, but the point is moot: Jimmy's record in world-class competition and his accomplishments as a coach and trainer speak for themselves, and lend great credibility to his advice. He also happens to be one of the few trainers in the world whose principles and beliefs concerning the training of horses and riders closely parallel my own. To be sure, we sometimes explain or express things a bit differently, but I consider Jimmy's basic concepts to be absolutely sound and based on reality.

I must add that as I read this book, I was struck by its very distinctive personal flavor. It sounds like Jimmy, and not some ghost writer, because, in fact, he wrote it himself. And though everybody in life is different, Jimmy is surely more different than most. You don't have to know him for very long to realize that he has a prodigious memory, not only for the battles of the Civil War, but also for jokes and one-liners of every persuasion. His sense of historical perspective gives him a great respect for tradition, but he is never too awed by it to dispute accepted precedents if they don't make sense to him, and he doesn't mince words.

All of these qualities show through in *Training the Three-Day Event Horse and Rider*, which is written in the inimitable Wofford style. Anyone who aspires to train or work with horses should be able to learn something from this wily horseman. I wholeheartedly recommend his splendid book to any eventer, young or old.

—Mark Phillips

Acknowledgments

THIS book would not be a reality without the help of several people. Bill Steinkraus had faith in me and made the process of writing a book as painless as possible. Joel Fishman and Frances Jones are responsible for polishing and condensing my sometimes awkward prose, for which many thanks. Brant Gamma took on the unenviable task of organizing my photos and illustrations, and the quality of her work shines through these pages. Becky Smith brought forth endless drafts and redrafts with expertise and enthusiasm. Merrilyn and Jeff Blue performed miracles in retouching old photos. My gratitude goes to Sharon Anthony, who knows now the true meaning of rough draft. And finally, thanks and love to my parents, Dot and Gyp Wofford, who gave me my start in the sport.

Training the Three-Day Event Horse and Rider

MY father died when I was quite young. I would like to have asked him what it felt like to walk down the ramp into a stadium full of 105,000 people for the final round of the 1932 Olympics— on a horse of somewhat dubious character. He and Babe were the alternates until a week before the Games, when the horse in front of them broke down. You can tell from Daddy's firm position here that he's determined to give it his best shot. Colonel John W. Wofford on the United States Army's Babe Watham, Olympics, Los Angeles, 1932.   U.S. ARMY

Introduction

THIS is a book about training three-day event horses and riders. While I believe that riders who are primarily interested in dressage or show jumping will find many things of interest here, my main focus will be on preparing horses and riders for three-day events at the various levels that exist in the United States today.

Although there is a fair amount of classical theory in this book, I have tried to be very concrete and to emphasize the nuts and bolts of riding. That way, you will have specific answers for the specific problems that any horseman is bound to run into during the training period. It takes a long time to develop a system for teaching three-day eventers that really works. I've been at it for thirty years now, and I hope to share what I've learned—the hard way—with you.

Many people make the mistake of seeking out successful competitors when they're looking for a trainer. Unfortunately, competitors frequently make terrible trainers, since their methods often are sharply influenced by the particular horses they happen to be riding at that time. Yet competitive results are so important to prospective students I thought I'd better give you a brief summary of mine.

I joined the USET three-day event team in 1965 and remained a member until 1985. During that time I won team and individual medals at two Olympics, one Alternate Olympics, and two World

*W*HEN you jump an enormous puissance wall, you have to be forward over the horse's shoulders, in order for the horse to clear the fence behind. Although Warren's lower leg has displaced slightly, his balance and his sympathetic hands have allowed Hollandia to show a nearly perfect bascule over an enormous fence. Notice the eerie mirror image in the tree line to the horse and rider's outline. Warren W. Wofford on Mrs. John W. Wofford's Hollandia, Rotterdam CSIO, 1961. JEAN BRIDEL DE L'ANNÉE HIPPIQUE

Championships. I also won the U.S. National Championship five times on five different horses.

A better measure of success, however, should be the students who have come out of my system. The majority of my income, over the past twenty-five years, has come from teaching event horses and riders around the country, especially in clinic situations. This has forced me to develop exercises and answers for the most common problems that I run across. It has been a rare U.S. international team that has not included at least one rider who got where he was by following the methods outlined in this book. Many of them appear in the photos contained in these pages, so you can judge for yourself. With only four exceptions, all the photographs in this book are either of my family or of my students.

Since any work of this nature is necessarily derivative, you also

UN on horseback comes in many different shapes and sizes. You should not get so focused on any particular field of activity that you cannot relax and enjoy a day on a wonderful plantation horse, following bird dogs in search of an elusive bobwhite quail. The smile on my wife's face shows you the enormous pleasure she gets from any sort of horse activity. Mrs. James C. Wofford on Mrs. C. Martin Wood's Perfect, Live Oak Plantation, Monticello, Florida, 1994. MRS. C. MARTIN WOOD, MFH

*M*Y sister-in-law, Dawn Palethorpe Wofford, who retired at a relatively early age, rode for the British Olympic team in 1956 and 1960. She was a natural rider, with little formal training, and could get the most incredible efforts out of her horses from the most unusual positions. You wouldn't teach anyone to sit over a square oxer, but look at the effort Paddy is making behind! I suspect that a technical coach would have pulled his hair out over this pair. When I asked her about it, she replied, "I always knew before I got to the fence whether my horse would jump it clean or not." Not many people are born with that sort of gift. Dawn Palethorpe Wofford on Earlsrath Rambler winning the Queen Elizabeth Cup, London, 1958.   FOTO TIEDEMANN HANNOVER

ought to know who has most influenced my riding career. I've been lucky to work with some incredibly talented horsemen. In the order of my making their acquaintance, they were: Col. John W. Wofford, Zygmunt "Bill" Bilwyn, Bert de Némethy, Stephan von Visy, Jill Fanning, Hector Carmona, Lars Sederholm, Major Joe Lynch, Colonel John Russell, and Jack Le Goff. Certainly the two people who had the most impact on my riding, however, were de Némethy and Le Goff. Anyone who ever heard their voices echo through the USET riding hall at Gladstone, New Jersey, knows the sound of genius at work.

If there's genius in this book at all, it derives from these great horsemen. My main contribution has been to distill their precepts in an easy-to-read, easy-to-apply format. It's impossible to thank everyone who had an effect on my riding and teaching. Suffice it to say that, if I ever watched you or your horse go, I learned something and, hopefully, applied it in my own career.

Because my development was uniquely affected by my family's involvement with horses, I'll also tell you a bit about my family background.

My father, Colonel John W. Wofford, rode in the 1932 Olympics at Los Angeles on the United States show jumping team. He later coached both the three-day event and show jumping teams to bronze medals at the 1952 Olympics in Helsinki, Finland.

My oldest brother, Jeb Wofford, won a bronze medal at those Olympics. My middle brother, Warren Wofford, is the only USET rider ever to qualify for both the show jumping and the three-day event teams, which he did in 1956. He then had the misfortune to pick the wrong discipline and went to the Olympics in Stockholm, Sweden, in 1956 as the show jumping alternate. Still, he was lucky enough to meet his future wife there, Dawn Palethorpe from Great Britain.

Dawn rode my mother's horse Hollandia (which was also Billy Steinkraus's mount in the 1952 Olympics) in the Rome Olympics in 1960 as a member of the British show jumping team. You can see that by the time I came along, it wasn't a question of *if* I was going to try out for the Olympics, it was a question of *when.*

The Wofford family's equestrian involvement is wider than just the Olympic disciplines. My favorite cousin, Billy Wofford, has ridden and trained numerous winners of races, both on the flat and over fences, including a winner of the Virginia Gold Cup and the

*I*F I ever have to jump a cross-country fence that no one has ever seen before, and my life depends on it, I want to be looking through the ears of Carawich.

Here I'm concentrating on getting away from the fence, making the first stride a galloping stride. I'm allowing my elbows to follow his mouth, while I stay behind him with my body. It is important that you land going the same speed that you took off with if you are going to make the optimum time around a big cross-country course. Because my leg is underneath me I will be able to take the shock of landing and continue galloping. The author on Carawich, Blue Ridge, Boyce, Virginia, 1978. GAMECOCK PHOTO

Timber Horse of the Year. As if that weren't enough, five members of my immediate family have been Masters of Foxhounds, including my wife Gail.

My family has always felt a debt to our sport and we have served in various capacities throughout the horse world. My father, Colonel Wofford, was a founder and the first President of the United States Equestrian Team. I have served as Vice President of the USET and recently retired as President of the American Horse Shows Association, the national governing body of horse sports in the United States.

My sister-in-law, Dawn Palethorpe Wofford, is currently President of the British Pony Clubs; and my brother Warren was Vice Chairman of the British Riding Club Association. At one point, among the three of us, we represented over 150,000 active riders in our various organizations. So our involvement starts to look more like an obsession than a hobby, and I don't really know what to say about that. I guess you can choose your hobbies, but your obsessions choose you.

𝒥F you are going to begin riding at an early age, you are going to need a good pony. Merrylegs was the best. She taught all three of my brothers and sisters how to ride and carried me on many a hair-raising expedition over the rolling grasslands at Fort Riley, Kansas. The author on Merrylegs, Rimrock Farm, Milford, Kansas, 1947.

THE dressage arena for the 1952 Olympic selection trials. My brother, J.E.B. (Jeb), was a member of the 1952 bronze medal team. You can tell by the background that we were not expecting a crowd at Rimrock Farm to watch the dressage phase. J.E.B. Wofford on Benny Grimes, Milford, Kansas, 1951.   ANDERSON STUDIO

1

The History and Development of the Three-Day Event

THE modern three-day event is the so-called triathlon of the horse world, but it hasn't always been this way, the format and requirements having changed over the years. The origins of the three-day event reach back over a hundred years. Originally the participants were all from the military, and events basically took the form of endurance rides, with no jumping or galloping involved.

To give you an idea of some of the distances that these horses and riders covered; in 1892 there was an endurance ride from Berlin to Vienna, a distance of 360 miles, which the winner covered in 71 hours and 26 minutes. Throughout the late nineteenth century many rides of this type took place. But after the turn of the century it became clear that such races had little value in preparing military horses and riders for combat. This occasioned the development of what the French called *"raids militaires,"* which were truly the fore-runners of three-day events as we know them.

The first three-day event that a modern rider would recognize took place at the 1912 Olympics in Stockholm, Sweden. The Olympic competition consisted of a long distance ride of 55 kilometers (33 miles) with a time allowed of four hours, which gave a speed of roughly 230 meters per minute. This was immediately followed by a cross-country test of 5,000 meters with a required speed of 333 meters per minute. There were no bonus points awarded for excess speed, although riders were penalized for exceeding the time allowed.

The horses were then given a rest day, following which they competed in a steeplechase test. This took place on a 3,500-meter racecourse over ten plain steeplechase fences at a required speed of 600 meters a minute. Again, there were no bonus points, but there were time penalties for going slower than the time allowed.

The following day was the show jumping phase, which spectators at the 1912 Stockholm games considered "easy." Then, on the final day, was the dressage test. It is interesting to note that the first three-day event already had a very complex scoring system and was spread out over five days. Our sport started out complicated and has remained so to the present day.

By the 1924 Olympic games in Paris the three-day event had evolved pretty much to its modern format. The only items worthy of notice are that a day's rest was allowed between each of the three tests—the dressage, the cross-country, and the jumping—and that the speed was slightly slower in the steeplechase, having been reduced to 550 meters per minute. In this general sequence the three-day event has continued to the present day.

It is interesting to contrast the 1912 program in the Stockholm Olympics with the 1992 Barcelona Olympics, eighty years later. The 1912 Olympics consisted of:

Day 1. Speed and endurance test
Day 2. Rest day
Day 3. Steeplechase
Day 4. Show jumping
Day 5. Dressage

The 1992 Barcelona Olympics consisted of:

Day 1. Dressage
Day 2. Dressage
Day 3. Speed and endurance test
Day 4. Show jumping

The distances covered on the speed and endurance test at Barcelona were:

Phase A — 6,000 meters
Phase B — 2,760 meters
Phase C — 8,000 meters
Phase D — 7,410 meters

In the United States we recognize three levels of three-day event competition. These are referred to, in ascending order of difficulty, as Preliminary, Intermediate, and Advanced. When these competitions are run under FEI (Fédération Équestre Internationale) regulations they are distinguished by means of a "star" system, which ranks the various levels with one to four stars. In the current United States rules, one star signifies Preliminary, two stars represent Intermediate, and three mean Advanced; four stars signify an event of unusual difficulty, often a Continental or World Championship event. Thus a CCI*** is a three-day event, run under FEI rules, at the Advanced level. Similarly, a Preliminary three-day event would be referred to as a CCI (Concours Complet Internationale) one-star (CCI*).

The heights, spreads, and speeds of the various levels are sequential, with the heights and spreads of the Advanced level coinciding with that required in the Olympics. The Olympics, World Championships, Pan American Games, and other continental championships are referred to as CCIO's. The "O," which stands for Officiel, signifies the official team nature of the competition. The same speeds, distances, heights, and spreads are used as in Advanced three-day events, but the allowed distances are longer.

Whatever the level, the same horse and rider must take part in all three disciplines—dressage, speed and endurance, and show jumping—and both must successfully complete all three parts of the competition. The preparation for one of these lower level three-day events will take months and, at the higher levels, years of participation in lower level events will be needed before the horse and rider are ready to confront the challenge provided by a 3- or 4-Star CCI. The necessary combination of technical skills and physical development does not happen overnight. But the long hours and the shared danger form a partnership between you and your horse that is not matched by any other sport in which horse and rider compete together.

DRESSAGE PHASE

*I*N the dressage phase the horse and rider execute a compulsory sequence of dressage movements. These movements are scored on a basis of 0 to 10 per movement, and the resulting total is then converted into penalty points. All of the remaining scoring of the three-day event is also done on a penalty basis. Thus, the horse and rider combination with the lowest total penalty points is the winner.

The dressage movements serve the same function for the three-day horse and rider as the compulsory figures do for gymnasts. That is, to make sure that the horse and rider are classically trained.

The horse should be calm and happy in his work. The test should show that the horse moves freely forward, that he cheerfully lengthens and shortens his stride at the almost invisible aids of the rider. His paces should always show energy and regularity. His outline should be steady and consistent, with the poll higher than the withers and the nose at or slightly in front of the vertical. At no time should the horse show that any part of his body is paralyzed by resistance. All of these requirements are difficult to achieve on a horse that is nearly racing fit. The courage, initiative, and seemingly limitless energy of a fit three-day event horse are difficult to reconcile with the obedience, calmness, and stability required by the dressage test.

The dressage movements required range from turns, halt, rein-back, lengthening and shortening, to simple lateral movements like leg-yielding. At the higher levels, the horse is required to perform half-pass; extension of the stride at the walk, trot, and canter; counter-canter; and more advanced transitions like extended canter to walk, medium walk to canter, and so on.

*M*Y cousin, Bill Wofford, is better known for his exploits as a steeplechase rider, but you couldn't find anyone sitting better on a big drop into water. When the splash subsides you're going to find Billy sitting right in the middle of his horse, looking for the next element, and in control of the situation. William G. (Billy) Wofford on Hominy Grits, Mumford Horse Trials, Moline, Illinois, 1981.

OURSE design has certainly improved over the last thirty-five years. When we walked this course in 1958, everyone thought this water jump was hard enough. Jeb is a bit too far forward here, but he's very secure, and obviously preparing for the next obstacle. Note Cheyenne Mountain in the background. J.E.B. Wofford on Benny Grimes, Colorado Springs Wofford Trophy, 1958. STEWART'S, COLORADO SPRINGS

SPEED AND ENDURANCE TEST

*T*HE most important part of a three-day event is the speed and endurance test, which is divided into four segments or phases, plus a ten-minute veterinary examination between the third and the fourth phase. The sequence and the naming of the phases is as follows:

The first segment, Phase A (sometimes referred to as Roads and Tracks) is a warm-up phase for the steeplechase. It is there to give the horse and rider the chance to trot and slow canter through the country for a short period of time. The rider should arrive one to two minutes early at the end of Phase A so that he will have time to adjust his girth and check his equipment to make sure that everything is ready for Phase B.

Phase B, the steeplechase, is the test of the horse's speed over jumps. It is carried out over eight to twelve plain brush fences, depending on the level of the competition involved and the length of the course. The speed will vary according to the level of competition, from 640 to 690 meters per minute. That may seem fairly rapid to the novice rider, but more experienced riders will realize that most racehorses condition their wind at 800 meters per minute, or the horseman's "two-minute lick." So this speed is within the capability of quite a few horses if they are well prepared.

Phase C is a longer Roads and Tracks section. Usually Phase C will be two thirds of the total distance of the Roads and Tracks while Phase A will be one third. As an interesting sidelight, usually the steeplechase will be about half the distance of the cross-country, while the penalty points are twice as severe on Phase B as they are on Phase D, .8 per second on Phase B, but only .4 per second on Phase D.

At the completion of Phase C, the horse and rider pass into the ten-minute veterinary examination, referred to in the three-day world as the "vet box." During this mandatory ten-minute rest period the horses are checked for soundness and fitness.

Their pulse, respiration, and temperature are taken and compared to the average for horses both at rest and under stress. Those horses that are passed by the Ground Jury are then allowed to go forward to the final phase of the speed and endurance test, the cross-country phase. This phase consists of anywhere from eighteen to thirty-six jumping efforts, depending on the level involved. Again, the speed and distance required will vary according to the level of the competition.

Horses that successfully complete Phase D will be supervised by a vet panel until the vets have satisfied themselves that the horse has come to no harm or distress during its exertions on the speed and endurance day. At that point the horse is released to return to the stables to prepare for the final day, the show jumping test.

SHOW JUMPING TEST

*T*HE show jumping test consists of a normal show jumping course, with heights and spreads similar in difficulty to moderate show jumping classes. The horse and rider that successfully complete a three-day event at any level can feel a justifiable sense of pride in their accomplishment. The three-day event is not for every horse. It requires courage, tenacity, perseverance, and both moral and physical strength from horse and rider.

At the same time, it is this element of difficulty that makes three-day eventing the most rewarding of all horse sports. No other endeavor that man and horse share can produce such a sense of unity. Only in a three-day event, with its shared risks, its hours of painstaking preparation, and its exhilarating sense of accomplishment upon completion, can riders produce a partnership with horses that transcends our ability to measure.

In recent years, the sport has come under intense and, to my mind, welcome scrutiny. Ours is a sport that any horseman can be proud of so long as we train our horses according to classic principles and rigorously enforce our rules as currently written. In the difficulty of the sport lie not only its charm and fascination, but its best protection. For in the final analysis a three-day event is not a test of speed and endurance, it is a test of character.

2

Selecting and Evaluating the Three-Day Event Prospect

TO start at the beginning, the first thing you need to go eventing is some kind of horse.

There is no such thing as a perfect three-day event horse. They come in all shapes and sizes. Two horses in the history of the Olympic Games have won two gold medals. Marcroix, a warmblood from Holland, was 18 hands high and won individual gold medals in 1928 and 1932. Charisma, the New Zealand Thoroughbred that won back-to-back gold medals in 1984 and 1988, could walk under the stick at 16 hands.

Other winning horses have run the gamut in size, shape, and lineage, but don't let this wide range of horses throw you off as you begin your pursuit of your three-day event horse. View it as an asset rather than a complication.

Before we describe the three-day event horse, I should mention that the best advice you will ever get about purchasing horses is, "Don't buy him if you don't like him the minute you see him." You may like a horse and then, later on, turn the horse down for soundness or performance reasons. But if you purchase a horse . . . suitable in every other respect . . . that you didn't like when you first saw him, you will never be happy with the horse. You will never make excuses for him, and you will never enjoy yourself as much as you would riding a horse that you fell in love with at first sight.

When going to look at a horse, look him in the eye. The look of eagles is alive and well in the horse world, and you should watch for it.

CONFORMATION

*T*HERE are some parameters that we can establish for the type of horse that will most likely be suitable for the requirements of the three-day event.

In general, the horse should appear symmetrical and proportional. The distance measured perpendicularly from the top of the withers to the bottom of the chest should be slightly longer than the distance from the bottom of the horse's chest to the ground. The distance from the point of the withers to the point of the shoulders should be as long as the horse's head. The withers and the croup should be the same height. You should be able to trace a straight line from the point of the buttock down through the point of the hock to the ground, and another line straight up through the foreleg to the top of the withers.

The horse uses its head and neck for balance. So the neck should be fairly long and directed about 45 degrees from the horizontal when the horse is attentively at rest. The neck should join a prominent withers. The topline should dip gradually from the withers to the back, which should then continue almost horizontally to the point of the croup. The loins, that is between the last rib and the point of the croup, should be short and well muscled. The horse should have a large, deep, and broad chest cavity to accommodate the lungs and the heart. The shoulder should slope from 60 to 55 degrees, or even less, in a horizontal plane.

The shoulder should join a long and rather upright humerus. An upright humerus has extensive forward movement, which allows free motion for galloping and jumping. The forearm should be long in comparison with the cannon bone, which will allow for a long stride and a minimum of knee action. The horse should not be "back" at the knee, knock-kneed, or bowlegged, but should form a straight line through the forearm and cannon bone to the ground. The pasterns should be of medium length and should slope at approximately 60 degrees from the horizontal in front. The foot should have broad heels, large tough frogs, with a concave sole. The front wall of the hoof should be parallel to the axis of the pastern.

The horse's croup should be long, inclined to 25 degrees from the horizontal on the topline, and be wide and muscular. The femur should be upright, close to perpendicular, and long, which allows for long strides. The stifle should be close to the abdomen and turned slightly outward. It should be at about the same height as the elbow. The tibia should be long relative to the cannon bone. The tibia should incline only slightly to the rear so that the hocks are not set out behind the horse. The hocks should have an open angle of about 160 degrees at the front face.

The horse should have broad, large joints and bones to provide attachment for the muscles and tendons of locomotion. Fine-boned horses are less desirable.

The eye of the horse should be limpid and calm. It should reveal an unquestioning acceptance of human presence. I place a great deal of importance on the visage of the horse as it reveals so much to me about the temperament and attitude of the horse in question.

The optimal size for an event horse is a much debated point. Colonel Harry D. Chamberlin, in his book *Training Hunters, Jumpers, and Hacks,* recommended 15 hands 3 inches. Some small event horses have been successful, although some small horses are at a disadvantage when required to carry 165 pounds at the Intermediate level and above. Competitors currently seem to prefer larger horses, 16 hands 2 inches and over, even though larger horses tend to have soundness and wind problems and may not be as athletic or durable as smaller horses.

Personally, I think that Colonel Chamberlin was right. Smaller is better for the three-day event horse.

There are also a few desirable deviations from the norm that are important for the event rider to understand. I think that a prominent, clearly defined withers, coupled with an exaggerated slope to the shoulders, is a definite beauty mark. Without appearing ewe-necked, the horse should be slightly high in front. This shape is a great source of confidence to you when thundering at a downhill vertical late in a long course; the horse will still feel high and balanced in front of you. In my own mind prominent withers and a sloping shoulder are the two most accurate, visual indications of the horse's jumping ability.

Another beauty mark, to me, is extreme depth in a horse's body versus extreme thickness. A deep, narrow horse many times is blessed with extraordinary cardiovascular capacities.

The horseman's adage is that, "a good horse will always have some length in him somewhere." Don't fault a horse too severely for the appearance of extra length in the back. Long-backed horses can jump the spreads required at the higher levels more easily. In addition to a slightly long back I like the horse to present a definite "wishbone" shape with an unusually long distance from the point of the hip to the point of the croup.

But probably, if I had to pick one thing that I had to hang my hat on, I would want the horse that I was going to buy to have a face that I would enjoy seeing poked over the stall webbing every morning, waiting for breakfast.

SOUNDNESS

*T*HERE are some soundness defects that the buyer should be aware of. Some of them, I think, you can live with and some of them not. At all times I try to avoid horses that have had injuries to the tendons and ligaments of the lower legs. These will usually come back to haunt you given the speed and stress of a three-day event, especially at the higher levels. My father always said "a bowed tendon will break your heart." I also try to avoid navicular and pedal osteitis. Nothing will cause the horse to lose his jumping form faster than landing on feet that hurt. Loss of form in horses that used to jump well can often be traced to a deterioration of the structure of the foot.

I also try to avoid horses with a history of azoturia. Azoturia is a very difficult condition to deal with. Although I have had some limited success in turning these horses around, the mental stress and strain worrying about whether the horse is going to get sick again make it seem easier to avoid purchasing the problem in the first place.

Horses with calf knees (also called "back at the knee") should be avoided at all costs. This aberration in their structure will cause chips and stress fractures, especially when landing over bigger jumps and drops. On the other hand, a horse that is slightly over at the knee usually is a better than average jumper. I have never found that this conformation defect led directly to any lameness. So it is one of the few conformation flaws that I can live with.

Also, if I have to choose, I will choose a horse that toes out rather than in, if the horse is not completely straight in front. If I had to choose a flaw behind, I would choose a horse that moves in a slightly narrow fashion rather than wide. Many good jumpers rope walk. Very, very few horses that straddle at the canter can jump well.

TEMPERAMENT

ECAUSE of the antithetical nature of the three-day event, the horse's temperament is of prime importance. It is difficult to produce the calm obedience required for a good dressage test when a horse is fit to do a 3,000-meter steeplechase and a 6,000-meter cross-country course. It takes a special type of horse to understand the difference between galloping at speed over fixed fences and a return to the show jumping arena on the third day where a sober, conservative approach is required in order to negotiate obstacles that knock down.

It can be somewhat difficult to evaluate temperament because the problems do not occur until the horse becomes fit. A horse that is hog fat and out of work during the winter may seem like a very easy ride. But six months later he can be a real handful for the rider who has never dealt with a fit horse before. So I think it is important to understand the relationship between fitness and temperament. Keep in mind that a careful examination of the horse's competitive record may give you a clue to any Jekyll and Hyde tendencies.

BREEDING

OR Preliminary three-day events a well-prepared horse of any breeding, given that he has the jumping ability, can successfully complete the event. Past that, as the rider promotes himself and his horse up the ladder, it becomes increasingly important that the horse have some Thoroughbred blood. Probably at the Advanced, World Championship, and Olympic level, it will be impossible for a horse to make the time over a modern event course without a vast majority of Thoroughbred blood running through his veins.

There has been in the recent past a trend toward European warmbloods because of their jumping ability and dressage paces. These horses do well at the lower levels, but they get tired and let you down at the more important, longer competitions. Therefore, I only recommend warmbloods, half-breds, and so on, to riders who are competing at the lowest levels. After that, I make every effort to be sure that my students are mounted on Thoroughbreds.

MATCHING HORSE AND RIDER

THE requirements for a rider looking for his first three-day event horse are different from an international rider seeking a new prospect. The needs of the rider who has never done a three-day event before are very simple: buy a horse that has already successfully completed a three-day event and come out of it sound.

If you are heading into your first three-day event, you are going to have enough on your mind just trying to remember the various complexities of the phases, rules, and so on. It will be a great source of comfort to you that your horse already knows how to do the test that you are placing in front of him.

After you have ridden in several three-day events you may wish to trade the horse in for something with more speed, movement, and scope. The requirements that you should keep in mind are as follows: no one ever got hurt in the dressage arena—your ego may be bruised by finishing last, but you are still safe and sound. And many times a clean and fast cross-country, plus a clean show jumping round, will move you up in the placings quite a bit. In other words, you can compromise and sacrifice some dressage performance. You can also accept a horse that rarely show jumps clean in a three-day event but always jumps. Five points out of the overall total can move you up and down a bit in the placings, but again, you are still safe and sound. At no time should the first-time three-day event rider be willing to compromise on the horse's cross-country and steeplechase jumping ability. The horse absolutely must jump safe and sane at the first attempt.

Later on, as you develop experience, you can start to ride horses that need help. For example, some may need skillful riding going into a water jump or require some fairly serious restraint on the steeplechase if they're to retain as much energy as possible for the later phases. But the first-time rider should not be presented with these problems. Buy a horse that, when presented with the obstacle, will get you safely to the other side without a lot of help from you.

If you are shopping for an Intermediate three-day event horse, the range of animals available to you becomes greater. For example, you can take a horse that has been spoiled in his show jumping shape and, through a system of intelligent gymnastic jumping, coupled with more proficient dressage riding, have an enormous influence on that horse's performance. But this should not be attempted by riders in their first season of three-day eventing. You'll have enough on your mind.

The more experience a rider has, the less the horse needs. For example, if you have ridden in several three-day events, find a young horse that has a season and a half of Preliminary, plus several Intermediate horse trials. With your additional experience, this is a nice sort of prospect to purchase and start preparing for a three-day event. Because of the qualification system these days, you should review the rule book and find out what it is that the horse must have done in the past in order to be qualified for the level of event you have in mind.

More experienced riders have quite a wide range of horses available to them. They can buy young, good-moving, athletic Thoroughbreds off the track. If their pocketbook is limited, they can go out and buy talented but extremely difficult horses that are competing on the circuit with every expectation that they can continue to ride that horse at that level of performance or better. Or they can take horses that possibly have had a history of stopping at ditches or stopping at water or whatever and turn that horse around. But again, this sort of purchase is for more experienced riders and should not be undertaken by riders going into a three-day event for the first time. In closing, buy a horse that fills all or most of the requirements contained in this chapter, but most of all buy him because you like him and enjoy working with him.

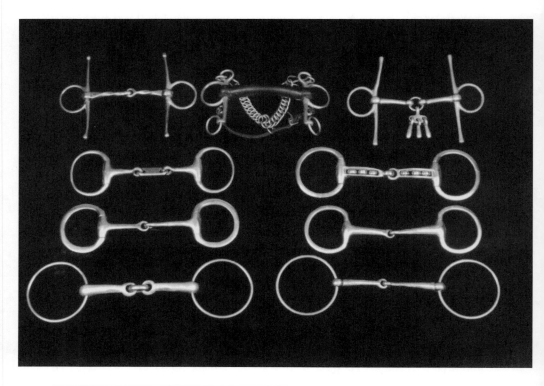

$\mathcal{M}$Y motto is "more bit, less rider." Experiment with one of these bits until you find the one that suits your horse, and then improve his dressage and your skills. I don't approve of hand-riding. There is a great temptation to substitute bits for training, but a sharp bit will always let you down just when the competition is the most important. Train your horse to carry himself, rather than relying on your hand.

BRANT GAMMA

3

Equipment for Horse and Rider

EQUIPPING THE HORSE

*N*OW that you have a horse suitable to go three-day eventing with, you'll need the correct equipment for all three tests. The connection between the rider's hand and the horse's mouth is the most important part of riding, and we had better start there.

The end result of classical riding is that the horse is perfectly balanced between the rider's hands and legs at all times. There is nothing in this statement that implies any form of compulsion. The horse should be in self-carriage throughout the three days of the event, including all four phases of the speed and endurance day.

Any gadget bit, or any bit which depends on pain and leverage rather than pressure, is a substitute for training. Substitutes will eventually let you down. Your best bet is to put on a simple snaffle, a flat caveson fitted loosely, and begin the training of your horse at this point. Obviously he will present difficulties to you. I doubt that you have been able to purchase a horse that was already perfectly trained. However, part of the fun of preparing three-day event horses is feeling them change and improve. If you will proceed in a logical and consistent fashion, you will be amazed at the progress you can make.

Horses' mouths fall into two general categories, either dry-mouthed or busy. "Dry-mouthed" horses hold the bit still in their mouth and usually make a concerted effort to lean on the rider's hands. A "busy-mouthed" horse continually plays with the bit, opening and closing his mouth, lifting or lolling his tongue, and usually tries to overflex. Horses that are dry-mouthed should be put in a loose-ring snaffle, which will provide some extra suppleness to the bit in the horse's mouth. Extreme cases can be dealt with at home by using a yearling or "keys" bit in order to promote mobility of the horse's jaw.

Horses that are already overly supple in their mouths and avoid contact by gaping their mouths or gnashing their teeth should use a flat-ring or egg-butt snaffle. This will produce more stability in the connection between the rider's hand and the bit in the horse's mouth. All horses will be one-sided to a greater or lesser extent. Extreme cases may be dealt with by using a double-jointed snaffle, either a French-link or a Dr. Bristol. Horses that loll or ball their tongue should have the bit placed one or two holes higher than usual in the mouth, to prevent them from getting their tongue over the bit.

Whatever your problem, resist the temptation to use a sharp bit in your day-to-day training. For example, if you find out that your horse goes very well in a Dr. Bristol, save that bit until the competition, and make yourself train the horse in a milder version at home. If a horse is exposed to the same bit every day, it soon develops defensive mechanisms. The rider who can deal with the problem at home in a milder bit, with less noseband, can then go to a competition, change from a flat-ring snaffle and caveson to a Dr. Bristol with a figure eight or drop noseband, and find that the horse remains in competition very much as it was at home. However, if you have already escalated the war of bits at home, you have no place left to go, and the horse will start to dominate the battlefield.

Whatever bit you select to compete in, make sure you look at the illustrations in the rule book to verify that the current rules allow the type of bit that you intend to use. Nothing is more upsetting than to be told by an official at the last moment that your bit is not legal. You will have to go borrow one from a friend ten minutes before you are due in the dressage ring, which can be disconcerting.

At the higher levels riders are allowed to use a double bridle. Some riders find that a double bridle solves many of their problems, especially stiffness at the poll and the jaw, and they begin to use the double bridle too much. If you find that your horse goes better in a double bridle than a snaffle, and it is legal for your level, the best thing you can do is hang your double bridle on a tack hook. Save it until you get to the next competition and continue to train your horse in a snaffle. It is very difficult to keep a horse coming truly forward when it is worked regularly in a double bridle. The new evasions that the horse develops will be infinitely more complex than merely stiffening its poll or its jaw.

To improve the training of your horse, teach him to respond to the signals of your seat and legs, not to avoid pain on the bars of his mouth. If all you want is a "head set," then by all means use a bitting rig. Within four or five days, you can create a horse that stands with a perfect head and neck position. But the art lies in teaching the horse to keep a light, following contact at all times, to carry itself, and to continue to produce that sort of result in competition.

Remember, using more bit is an admission that either your horse, you, or both, are not yet properly trained to the level of competition. Humans being human, you will probably continue to use severe bits. But at least be realistic about what it tells the world about your riding.

CROSS-COUNTRY BITS

IF three-day event riders have a tendency to over-bit their horses in dressage, they have an absolute compulsion to over-bit their horses for the cross-country test. Remember that you are in a race across country against the clock. Very, very few steeple-chasers or timber racehorses ever run in anything more than a snaffle. You don't *want* to slow the horse down—you want the horse to make the time so that you do not incur further penalties. The further up the ladder (from Preliminary to Advanced) one goes, the more difficult it is to avoid time faults and the more essential it is that you ride the horse in a plain snaffle.

In theory every time you touch the horse's mouth you shorten the stride. So you would like the horse to go on as soft a hold as possible and to approach the jumps at as quick a pace as safety will allow. The speed at which three-day event horses go appears quite rapid to riders who have never done any steeplechasing or point-to-pointing. Before you finally decide that your horse really and truly (no matter what any coach says) is running away with you, go to work for a racehorse trainer. Spend some time learning to deal with fit racehorses. You will find that, after ninety days of practice, you can control the speed of most horses you are given to deal with. The beneficial effect to your fitness will be enormous. The beneficial effect to your technical training will be beyond measure, because you will become convinced that it is the horse's balance that controls the speed and not the pressure of your reins on his mouth.

This lesson is in the same category as telling novice riders, "Don't pull on a horse that is trying to run away or he will run away." It doesn't make sense at the time, but, sooner or later, all of us learn this technique and are then able to deal with horses that, even a short time before, were beyond our capabilities. The same lesson exists in riding cross-country at speed. It is up to you to learn it.

BITS FOR SHOW JUMPING

*T*HREE-DAY event horses get tired and flat after their exertions on the speed and endurance test. Because of this and because the duration of the competitive phase is so short, you can get away with a sharper bit than you could during the dressage or cross-country. Again, however, you must remind yourself that you are solving your training problems by causing discomfort to your horse's mouth, not by improving its training.

Don't be fooled by the fact that your horse jumps well in a certain type of gadget bit. Riders start to think that, because their show jumping has improved, they can take this apparatus out on the cross-country. The problem is that, once the horse "burns through" in its mouth in a gadget bit, it becomes much worse than it would be if it were just pulling strongly against a regular snaffle. Past a certain point, pain on the bars of the horse's mouth creates a numb condition. At this point the horse truly is dangerous and out of control. The answer in the long run is always more training, not more bit.

Usually the rider in the show jumping ring wants a bit which will elevate and lighten the forehand of the horse. For this reason I use slow twist snaffles, Dr. Bristols, and mullin-mouths in order to help the rider keep the horse together for a short period of time on the final day.

I suppose there are horses that need to go in a gag snaffle. But the problem with gag snaffles, as with most other forms of gadget bits, is that they work! They work by magnifying the effect of the rider's hand on the horse's mouth. This is a wonderful condition if you can guarantee to me that you will never make a mistake with your hands during the competition. If you can make such an assurance, then you can use any sort of bit that you like, and the horse's mouth will continue to be protected.

If you are human like the rest of us, you are going to make mistakes, and these mistakes will be terribly magnified in the horse's mouth, especially by any form of lever-action bits such as kimberwickes, pelhams, or the worst of the bunch, gag snaffles. Ride your horse in a simple snaffle and train him to answer the signals of your hands and legs, and you will start to produce the results that you want through training and education rather than through pain and discomfort.

NOSEBANDS

*T*HERE are four basic types of nosebands. In their order of desirability they are (1) caveson, (2) sliding figure eight, (3) dropped, and (4) flash.

The old joke in the warm-up ring is that you can never be too rich, too thin, or have your noseband too tight. I prefer that you ride with a milder bit and a tighter noseband. You will do less damage to the horse's mouth and interfere least with the horse's training. Just as by changing bits before a competition, you can achieve a beneficial, short-term effect before a competition by putting the next most restrictive noseband on the horse and closing his mouth. Short term, this will cause the horse to become more sensitive to your hands and an attractive result can be achieved even in competition. But, just as with sharp bits, you must not fool yourself into believing that the training of the horse has improved. Rather, the restraining of the horse has improved and you will have to do some remedial training after the competition.

1. The plain *caveson* is the noseband that the horse should train in the vast majority of the time.

The caveson should be fitted two fingers below the cheekbones and with one to two fingers' separation at the jaw so that the caveson rests lightly but basically does not restrain theaction of the horse's jaw.

2. I specify a *sliding figure eight* so that, when the noseband is adjusted properly, the pressure is equalized above and below the bit. This noseband is excellent for horses that take a one-sided hold or cross their jaw in an attempt to avoid the rider's control. The sliding nose piece allows the noseband to be fit to a wide variety of horses and makes sure that the pressure is equalized top and bottom.

3. The *dropped noseband,* when correctly fitted, is a good tool to keep the horse's mouth closed. However, you may have to experiment if your horse has a slightly unusual shape to the bridge of his nose or the length of his mouth. Only experimentation will produce a dropped noseband that fits correctly. This noseband is quite effective against horses that open their mouths. It does not give the control that a figure eight does if the horse also crosses its jaw.

4. My least favorite of these nosebands is the *flash.* The flash is basically an inefficient figure eight. It is very difficult to get the pressure equalized. It is also difficult to adjust the caveson part of the flash correctly and still exert any beneficial pressure with the dropped noseband. If the dropped noseband is put on tight enough to have an effect, it will drag the caveson down in an unsightly fashion. If it is put on looser, then it is not having an effect and you would be better off trying one of the more efficient types of nosebands. Nosebands, like all other forms of riding equipment, are subject to fads. You should avoid the use of equipment just because a famous rider uses it. Analyze what it is that your horse is doing to evade you and what equipment is legally available to you to help you solve your problems during the competition. Better yet, correct the problem with good training.

MARTINGALES

*M*ARTINGALES come in three basic varieties—standing, running, and Irish. The most common is the running martingale. Fit the martingale so that the ring, when pulled straight up, comes at or above a horizontal line drawn from the horse's hip. Especially when jumping cross-country, too short a running martingale can cause the horse to drop his hind legs when his mouth comes up and hits the restraining action of the martingale. The running martingale should be two holes longer on cross-country day than for show jumping.

Standing martingales are extremely useful in the training of young horses, but because they are not allowed in competition, I discontinue their use as soon as the horse's head and neck become stabilized enough to be safe.

Irish martingales are basically two connected rings that keep the reins separated and underneath the horse's neck. When I asked an Irishman, "Why Irish martingales?" he said, "Sure, if you have a rough fence, it keeps the reins from going over 'is head and neck." My thinking at the time was that if the horse was that bad a jumper, I wasn't going to ride it!

Martingales are overrated in their importance. They can, occasionally, help with horses that are difficult to turn and control. But you should also realize that, although it can be an evasion every time a horse brings his head and neck up, he's also putting weight into his hindquarters. A skillful rider should be able to take advantage of this in some fashion.

REINS AND GLOVES

*T*HE best reins to use for all three phases are leather reins covered with rubber hand grips. The width of the reins is determined by two criteria, the first being strength of the horse. The more the horse pulls, the wider the reins should be, as this spreads the pressure over your fingers better. If the reins are thin on a puller, you get the sensation that you have a wire biting into your hands. Your hands will become sore and tired much sooner than if you ride with wider reins. However, if your hands are quite small you should consider using a thinner rein so that your hands do not feel completely filled up. A slightly thinner rein may be easier for you to manipulate.

Whatever the width of the rein that you choose, make sure it is a dark, conservative color and not one of the bright new nylon or multicolored reins that are coming out on the market. All of your equipment should be serviceable but none of it should call attention away from the performance of the horse.

Get used to riding in gloves all the time. If you expect the horse to produce a large amount of lather on his neck, or if you are riding in the rain, then I would suggest that you use gloves which have rubber covering on the fingers and palms in order to control the reins. You really have to be riding in a downpour before you should change to web reins with leather stops on them. These reins invariably place your contact either too short or too long. It is quite difficult to adjust web reins to the correct length, and you will never feel entirely at home in them. In addition, because of the leather stops on the reins, web reins can be very difficult to "slip" when you're going over drops or into water, as your fingers tend to catch on the leather stops. Whatever reins you use, make sure that you check the stitching quite often both at the buckle and at the end of the reins where the reins connect to the bit. This is a major site of equipment failure.

BREASTPLATES

*T*HERE are three basic types of breastplates that you can use in order to keep the saddle in the correct place above the withers. Three-day event horses are especially prone to having the saddle slip back. As they become fit, they lose a great deal of the fatty tissue over the withers, and the clearance and placement of the saddle will start to change.

It is a rare three-day event horse that does not have a little scar tissue on his withers, because most riders learn this lesson the hard way. If you are getting your horse three-day event fit for the first time, remember to keep a close eye on the adjustment of your saddle as you get within the last thirty to forty days of the event. The body of the horse will start to change after the speed work begins.

There are three types of breastplate that the rider can use. I prefer that they be used in this order:

1. *Polo breastplate.* This is the breastplate that comes perpendicular around the shoulder with a neck strap above and fastens with a loop around the girth. You should have a saddler sew a small loop on the front of the breastplate. A running martingale can then be threaded up through this loop, thus doing away with the need for a second neck strap if you use a running martingale. I have found this to be the most efficient arrangement.

2. The second most efficient breastplate is a *loop breastplate,* which merely clips to one of the D-rings on the front of the saddle, comes under the neck, back up the other side, and clips again. Because the breastplate does not oppose the action of the shoulder directly, I do not think that this keeps the saddle in as secure a place as a polo breastplate, but I think it does do some good, and certainly the convenience is a factor. I don't think that you should use a running martingale attachment to a loop breastplate. Since the loop breastplate is attached only at the saddle, it is loose under the neck, and a running martingale won't fit correctly.

3. *Hunting breastplates* are probably the most traditional. However, the action of the horse that makes the breastplate keep the saddle in place is the forward motion of the shoulder. The shoulder pushes against the breastplate, which pulls the saddle forward into place over the horse's withers. If you have a strap which remains parallel to the horse's shoulder, the horse is not going to tend to act against the breastplate, and therefore the saddle is going to slip back until it does connect against the shoulder. So I prefer the polo breastplate because it opposes the action of the shoulder directly and keeps the saddle over the withers.

Hunting breastplates have an additional disadvantage to my mind, and that is that it is difficult to have a running martingale attachment which is adjustable enough to fit a wide variety of horses. What I find is that you must have a hunting breastplate and a martingale attachment for each horse, and many times you must have a longer attachment to go cross-country for each particular horse and then a slightly shorter attachment for show jumping. If your horse needs a breast-plate, use a polo breastplate.

SADDLES

*I*F you have progressed far enough in your riding to be attempting a three-day event, then you should by now have three saddles. The ideal situation is to have a saddle for each of the tests—dressage, cross-country, and stadium jumping. It is possible

*I*F you use the wrong equipment, you will get the wrong result. For example, when you do dressage in a show jumping saddle, this is the shape that you will wind up in—legs too far forward, back round, slightly overflexed. The author on Kilkenny, World Championships, Punchestown, Ireland, 1970. CLIVE HILLS

that a saddle can be suitable for two tests out of the three and that you can then have a separate saddle for the third test. The most common combination saddles are saddles which are suitable for dressage and show jumping, or show jumping and cross-country. The requirements of dressage and cross-country are too disparate. Single-purpose saddles are far superior to combination saddles.

View with suspicion the "all-purpose" claims of some saddle makers. The very thing that makes a saddle suitable for one discipline will make it unsuitable for another discipline. As you progress up the sequence of three-day events, all your equipment must become more and more specialized. "All-purpose" saddles are no-purpose saddles.

The dressage saddle should have a deep seat with the deepest part of the seat quite close to a vertical line drawn from the stirrup bar down through the stirrup leather. As the speed of the horse increases and the stirrup length gets shorter, the deep part of the saddle must move farther back. Thus, a saddle which is suitable for

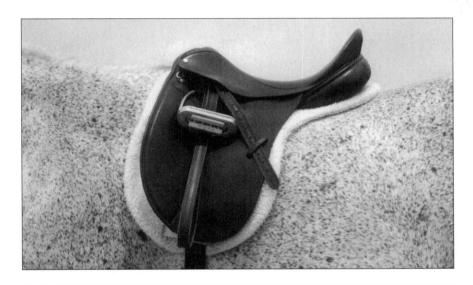

IT'S a poor carpenter that blames his tools; but by the time you are ready to go in a three-day event, you should have one saddle for each discipline. Make sure that your dressage saddle has a deep seat with the low part of the saddle well forward toward the stirrup bars so that you can easily sit above your feet. BRANT GAMMA

cross-country work will put you badly behind the motion if you let down your stirrups and attempt to do dressage. Saddles vary enormously in their construction and measurement, and you must try quite a few before settling on one that is suitable for your horse and yourself.

The cross-country saddle should have its skirts cut well forward to allow for shorter stirrups on the steeplechase phase. The low point of the seat should be well behind the stirrup bars. Then when you sit down in the approach to a fence, you will not feel tipped forward by the cantle of the saddle.

For cross-country the rider would like to maintain a close contact with the horse's shoulders and thus, excess stuffing under the thigh and knee is not desirable. In addition the knee roll should stop at the point of the knee and not continue down the skirt of the saddle. Long knee rolls cause the knee to open and slide backward in the landing phase of the jump.

If you have the same build that I do, then weight is a problem in the cross-country phase. There are specialty saddles that can be obtained of a very light weight, ten pounds or less, and this can be a great benefit to your horse, as some heavier saddles can weigh as much as twenty-five pounds.

The best show jumping saddles are the flat saddles, Hermès and Hermès imitations, which give the rider a close contact with the knee and lower leg and a neutral seat on which to sit in the approach to the jump. Expert observers comment on the lovely lower leg position of most American show jumping riders. You will find that 99 percent of those riders ride in a flat saddle. Saddles which are overstuffed in the knee roll area will cause you to lose your lower leg position while jumping. Here, as in so much of riding, less is more.

GADGETS

*N*O matter how much trainers may decry the use of gadgets, you are going to use them in the training of your horse anyway, so you might as well learn how to do as little damage as possible, and maybe even improve your horse on a short-term basis.

In general, all gadgets should be used to make the horse long, low, and slow so that the reins become light and the paces become slow and round. From that shape, you can use your leg to increase the engagement of the horse and thereby increase the elevation.

If, at the end of the work period, you can loosen the gadget or the draw-reins, and your horse, while not as good as under duress from the gadget, has improved from the way that it started out at

A SADDLE designed solely for cross-country. Notice the extra forward flap and the slightly higher cantle. The low part of the saddle is much farther back than for the close contact, show jumping saddle. When you shorten your stirrups, your seat bones move farther back in the saddle.

The horse is tacked as for cross-country. Note the knot in the reins, and the polo breastplate. If a running martingale is desired, you can have your saddler stitch a loop on the front of the polo breastplate. You will then have both a breastplate and a running martingale without the disadvantages of the extra neck strap. The lightweight irons should not be used unless you have a problem with weight, as they tend to make you fix your ankle. The loops on the girth are for a surcingle in case you use a weight pad. BRANT GAMMA

the beginning of the period, you can call that progress. But you must always check at the end of the work to make sure that you are using the gadget to put the horse in self carriage rather than to force the horse into elevation and collection. Used skillfully gadgets can shortcut training methods. Used improperly they ruin horses very quickly.

I have used the following gadgets on various types of horses and set them down here for your consideration:

1. *Draw-reins from the saddle,* sometimes called German reins or running reins. These reins are used to reinforce the action of the rider's hand. They should not be used on a horse with a tendency to lower his head and neck. These reins can cause a horse to overflex very quickly. Once a horse learns that habit it is difficult to correct. Used for short periods of time on horses that are extremely rigid in their jaw, however, they can help the rider achieve a breakthrough.

2. *Draw-reins from the girth,* also referred to as French reins. These reins are used on horses that resist in their withers and stargaze, and should be employed to show the horse the way to the ground. These reins should be adjusted so that they act only when the horse comes above the bit. Then, as soon as the horse yields at the poll and the withers, the reins become slack. This is my favorite gadget as riders will probably do the least damage with this gadget as with any.

Like any aid that magnifies the effect of the rider's hand, draw-reins are a razor blade in a monkey's hand; but adjusted anywhere close to correctly, they will probably produce as little overbending as any of the gadgets.

3. The *hand-Gogue.* This is a longer draw-rein, 18 to 24 inches longer on each side than a normal draw-rein. It starts at the girth, goes to a ring at the corner of the browband, drops down through the bit, and then comes back to the rider's hand. This gadget can be used for horses that are above the bit and therefore give their riders difficulty in keeping them in a steady frame. The hand-Gogue spreads out the poll and bit pressure so that the rider is better able to place the horse's head and neck. Here, as in the use of all of the gadgets, the emphasis must remain on the closing of the rider's leg on the horse's

sides and not on the stronger action of the reins on the horse's mouth or poll.

4. The next gadget that I am familiar with is a ***chambon.*** This is a rein or a cord which runs from between the horse's legs to a ring at the corner of the browband, and down to the bit. Care must be used when introducing this gadget to horses. Young horses or horses that are very resistant in their topline have an unfortunate tendency to flip over backward if the chambon is put on too tightly too soon. Introduce the horse to this gadget by stages. Use it mostly at the trot, as an exercise

A GOOD illustration of a close contact saddle, designed solely for the show jumping phase. Saddle design and construction play a large part in your ability to maintain your position. Look at quite a few models before you finally purchase a saddle, and be sure to discuss the saddle with your trainer, or a more experienced rider. If you plan to go to a three-day event, you will need a saddle designed specifically for each phase. BRANT GAMMA

to strengthen the horse's loins and increase the roundness and engagement of the step behind. Too much work at the canter in the chambon will give your horse a four-beat canter.

5. The final gadget that I use is a pair of *elastic side-reins.* These can be used to introduce riders to the concept of having a horse on the bit. For our purposes, the experience and expertise of the rider should be beyond this point. Mostly, elastic side-reins should be used when longeing the horse. In that case, care must be taken to allow the outside rein to be a couple of holes longer in order to promote the natural bending of the horse's body. Remember that any work on a longe line is extremely concentrated and you should, in effect, double the time that a horse spends. For example, twenty minutes on the longe line, due to the intensity of the circling and possibly the effect of the gadget in use, is equal to forty minutes of exercise

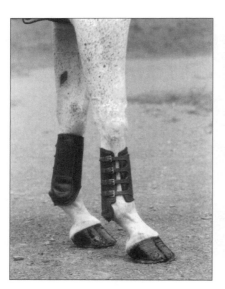 

I PREFER leather galloping boots, lined with foam rubber as illustrated here. Use boots that have a tongue and buckle closure, rather than Velcro or clasps. The latter will, invariably, come undone in tall grass or water. Coat the leather with waterproofing paste and your galloping boots will return from the cross-country course as dry as they went out. BRANT GAMMA

under the saddle. Sessions such as this should be used judiciously.

Make a habit of removing the gadget, side-reins, or draw-reins toward the end of the work period. Watch the horse for a few moments, or ride the horse yourself in order to evaluate its ongoing training.

Remember that gadgets give you a false effect. Many times when you go to a competition you are in for a rude shock. You will suddenly find that you have been using the gadget to support the horse rather than using the gadget to train the horse to support himself. Having said all this, no amount of warning is going to keep you from using artificial aids. Go ahead and experiment . . . just remember when you get in trouble, the reason for that trouble. You do not have a horse that is necessarily resistant, you have a horse that is untrained. That is your fault, not the horse's. Deal with it by training, not coercion.

RIDER'S EQUIPMENT

*R*EAD the rule book to see what the current rules allow and require for each of the three phases. Some of the dress rules for the dressage phases are fairly complex, while rules concerning headgear on cross-country are quite specific. Make sure that you comply with them. Once you are sure that you have followed the dress rules, then it is up to you. I prefer dark colors for your riding coat, neutral colors for britches, and black boots for the dressage and show jumping competition.

In the cross-country phase the rider can be a bit more colorful, but I still like to see the rider avoid having "matching everything." Matching helmet, shirt, gloves, breastplate, polo bandages, tail wraps, and saddle pads may be cute but they are not desirable at a high-class three-day event. The rider should not do anything to call attention away from the performance of the horse. Quiet, understated colors, a minimum of color coordination, flat leather work in the breastplate, martingale, and noseband, and a polished appearance are best.

4

Dressage

THE DRESSAGE POSITION

THINK of the dressage position as two straight lines. The first is a line vertical to the ground from your ear, through your shoulder, to your hip, to your heel. The second straight line is formed by the contact from your elbow to the horse's mouth. You should keep yourself in this framework at all times. There are other ways of describing this position . . . "the rider appears to sit above his feet" or "the rider's body forms a vertical line at a right angle to the horse's back." Whatever the description, your success is directly related to your dressage position.

THE BODY

THE foundation of your dressage position is the three-point seat. These three points are the two seat bones and the pubic bone. Your seat bones should be in the deepest part of the saddle with your pubic bone against the pommel. Your shoulders should be drawn well back, chest forward, and eyes straight ahead. You should keep an arch in the small of your back. The arch in the small of the back is essential. This is the shape that allows the horse to carry you without effort. If you sit on three points then you are sitting on a

𝒜 GOOD position at the halt. Notice the vertical line formed between the rider's ear, shoulder, hip, and heel. Her reins, however, are too long, causing her wrists to break. There is a correct arch in the small of the rider's back. All in all, a good working position. Anne Kontos on Go with the Flow, Fox Covert Farm, Upperville, Virginia, 1993. BRANT GAMMA

tripod which is stable in every direction. When you maintain an arch in the small of your back, you will be carried by the flow of the horse's motion rather than by the grip of your lower legs, whatever the direction of the horse's motion.

THE LEGS

*F*ROM the hips your legs should hang straight down, close to the horse's sides but relaxed. You should ride on the flat of your inner thigh, and your knee should be well down in the saddle without gripping. From the knee down, your lower leg should lie close to the horse's side, falling into the groove directly behind the girth. You should have the feeling, at any time, that you can take your knee and lower leg away from the saddle without disturbing either your position or the flow of the horse's motion.

Do not attempt to ride with your stirrups too long. If you must make a compromise in your position, you should sacrifice sensitivity for stability. The slight loss of a delicate leg aid will be more than compensated for by the feeling of confidence that comes from security in the saddle with a shorter stirrup.

You should feel the tread of the stirrup on the ball of your foot. The heel should always be carried lower than the toe as this is amajor shock-absorbing mechanism. However, locking the ankle down is as bad as standing on your toes. Keep your thigh bone, knee, shin, and foot in the same line. Allow this line to form a slight angle away from the horse's body. It is more important to keep the weight of the leg distributed equally over the tread of the stirrup than it is to keep the foot parallel to the horse's body.

HANDS AND ARMS

*T*HE position of your arms should form a straight line to the horse's mouth. Your thumbs should be on top of the reins, turned slightly in from the vertical with the elbows close to the

ABOVE LEFT

*A*N incorrect dressage position caused by rounding the lower back. The minute the arch in the small of your back is reversed, you lose your three-point seat. The minute you lose your three-point seat, you must grip with your hands, knees, and heels, causing the distinctive false position shown here. Fox Covert Farm, Upperville, Virginia, 1993. BRANT GAMMA

ABOVE RIGHT

*T*HERE is a fair amount of behind-the-scenes merriment when you try to get a good rider to sit in a bad position. Anne Kontos's face shows that she is uncomfortable with a perched seat, upper body too far forward, exaggerated arch in the small of the back, heels too far down, no leg contact, and knees off the saddle. Avoid this position at all costs. Fox Covert Farm, Upperville, Virginia, 1993. BRANT GAMMA

body. The forearm, the wrist, and the fingers will form a natural and direct extension from the elbow to the bit.

Note that this line will change as the training of the horse proceeds. As the elevation increases, the forearm of the rider will be carried higher above the withers. The straight line should bemaintained, however. The position of the hand is not determined by some artificial measurement but rather by the state of training of the horse. A very green horse will naturally carry his head and neck quite low. This is to be encouraged rather than discouraged, but you must compensate for this by riding with an extremely low hand position. In highly collected horses the forearm of the rider may actually be above the horizontal, yet still show a straight line from the elbow to the horse's mouth.

It is a misnomer to say that riders have good hands. Good riders have good elbows and good shoulders. The range of motion in the hands is limited. They can either squeeze or release the reins. The elbows and shoulders create the elastic feel that you seek.

When analyzing a rider's dressage position, I concentrate on the foundation of the seat. If the foundation of the rider's seat has a flaw—*for example,* sitting on the coccyx instead of the pubic bone to form the third point—other problems will appear. A rider riding with a round back and his waist dropped behind the motion will drop his head and neck, and grip with his hands and knees in an attempt to keep from being left behind the motion. Critical comments directed at correcting the head and neck position or softening the leg position will be wasted until the rider resumes a correct three-point position in the saddle.

If you wish to improve your dressage position, you have several means at your disposal. The most beneficial is to ride without stirrups. It is uncomfortable work at first, but the benefits will soon become apparent. Cross your stirrups over the pommel, find the balance point of the saddle, and sit there softly and quietly, always in harmony with the horse's motion. If necessary, hold the pommel with your outside hand.

Probably the best means of developing a secure, independent dressage position is through a series of longe line lessons and exercises. Following is a series of exercises that you can go through when working on the longe. You should ride the horse with side reins and the longe line, but no reins or stirrups. You will find that the horse's paces and movements will improve as soon as you adopt a balanced, harmonious position on the horse's back.

LONGE LINE EXERCISES

*Y*OU should practice the following exercises in a controlled situation with a horse that will carry you quietly, without shying or spooking, so that you can concentrate on your position rather than on your security.

Whenever you are not engaged in one of these exercises, carry your inside forearm behind you at waist level. Use your outside hand on the pommel to pull yourself forward and down in the saddle. Great care should be taken that, while performing one of these exercises, other parts of your body do not move. This is a true test of your independent seat. All of these exercises can be done at the walk, trot, or canter. Obviously, your experience and fitness will determine just how far you can go each day.

Throughout the lesson, let the legs hang straight from the hip. Do not lift the toes as this will cause the muscles around the knee to become stiff and tense. You will have to keep reminding yourself to let your legs down, as there is a tendency to grip and tighten in the knee and hip as the lesson progresses.

1. Roll your ankles in a circle so that the toes of one foot point straight toward the ground and the toes of your opposite foot point as far up as your joint conformation will allow. Do this four or five times on each side.

2. Keeping the knee straight, swing one leg forward over the knee roll. Bring the opposite leg back behind the skirt of the saddle. Do not disturb the upper body or twist the shoulders. This is an excellent exercise to develop the suppleness of your hip joints.

3. Reach behind your leg and pull your toe back with your hand until your heel touches your buttocks. This will stretch the hip joint and the top of the thigh.

4. Bring your arms straight out from your shoulders with the palms facing the ground. Now imagine that there is a string running from your palm to your ankle bone. Try and move your ankle up that string, one leg at a time. Do not bend the knees and make sure that your toes turn in toward the horse and not away from him. Again, do not disturb the upper body position while moving one leg or the other. It is quite common to get a sharp pain in the hip when doing this movement. Don't fight it, relax, go to the other side, and come back to this side. In a few days the hip joints will adapt and become more flexible.

5. Extend your arms to the sides at shoulder height, palms facing the ground. Turn back until you can see the opposite hip of the horse. Then, smoothly in rhythm with the pace of the horse, turn until you can see the other hip of the horse. Repeat this movement several times. Concentrate on keeping your head centrally located above your three-point seat; do not lean, do not allow your legs to change position or your arms to droop.

6. Extend both arms straight down at your side, palms facing the rear. Now bring one arm up behind the other in a windmill fashion, forward, up, over, and back down again. Reach as far up at the top of the circle as you can with your arm. Reach as far back as you can before turning the arm back down to your side. Keep this movement smooth and in rhythm with the horse's step. Do not rush through this exercise. Again, it is important that the head remain still above your three-point seat throughout this exercise.

7. Make two fists and alternately throw punches straight forward toward the horse's ears. Do not move your upper body, only your arms and shoulders. Make sure that your arm reaches full extension and that you feel a slight pulling sensation in the shoulder joint.

8. Again, both arms extended, palms facing the ground. Cross the arms in front of you, keeping them horizontal, then swing them back as far as they will go. Let them bounce forward and then swing them back behind you again. Do not duck your head and neck or lower your hands behind you as

*N*OTE the same relationship of the rider's upper body as in the photograph at the halt—a vertical line from ear to shoulder to hip and heel, and a straight line from the elbow to the horse's mouth. The legs are close without gripping. Both horse and rider present an attractive outline. Fox Covert Farm, Upperville, Virginia, 1993. BRANT GAMMA

you do this exercise. Keep your arms in the same horizontal plane throughout the exercise. From the snap, crackle, and pop that you will hear in your neck and shoulders, you will understand why I call this exercise "Rice Krispies."

There are two more exercises that I use for more advanced students. Again, these two exercises can be done at the walk, trot, or canter, but probably the emphasis here should be on the canter.

9. Cross your arms in front of your chest. Keeping the seat bones on the saddle, collapse forward until you touch your chin to the horse's mane. Now relax back until you touch the back of your head to the horse's croup. Then, using only your stomach muscles and your knee grip, come forward into a normal position again. You should be able to repeat this at least five times.

Done at the canter, the movement should take place in three strides—forward to the neck (1), back to the croup (2), and upright (3).

10. At the walk take the pommel with the right hand, bring the left knee to your chest, and swing the left heel over the pommel. You should now be sitting in an offside sidesaddle position. Hold the cantle with the left hand, press on the left seat bone, close the outside leg, and ask for a walk to canter transition. Maintain your position by a strong grip with the hand on the pommel. While the horse remains in the canter, bring the left knee to your chest, return that leg to the left side of the horse, reverse your hands, bring the opposite knee to your chest, and then across the mane until you are in sidesaddle on the near side.

This is an excellent exercise for supplying the hip joint. It will also prove to you that you do not need to grip in order to maintain your dressage position. By placing both knees on the same side of the horse it becomes impossible for you to grip with your legs, and you must learn to sit on three points instead.

All of these exercises are beneficial. All of them should be done under supervision and in an enclosed area. Remember that longeing is a very fatiguing exercise for the horse, and you should double the amount of time that you have been on the longe in order to measure the amount of work the horse has done. Twenty minutes on a longe line is like forty minutes of regular exercise for the horse.

These exercises should be done for at least five days in a row, about twenty minutes per session. You will have some success at first, but you will notice a slight stiffening each day until the fourth or fifth day when your body will start to adapt. If you have the time and the facilities, obviously, two weeks of longe lessons are better than one week. But even a day stolen here or there will help you improve your dressage position greatly.

The easiest way to improve your position is to work with a knowledgeable instructor. These individuals see riders on a regular basis. Many riders display similar flaws that are easily corrected by suggestion. The time and money spent in a lesson are well worth it. A good instructor can save you endless hours of heartache struggling to achieve a feeling neither the horse nor you truly understands.

I have often thought that one could take a layman off the street, dress him in riding clothes, place him on a horse, and verbally push him around until he achieved an attractive position in the saddle. But this position would be attractive only as long as the horse remained still. The moment the horse moved off, the novice would dissolve into terror, showing all of the symptoms of the novice rider. Only hours of long, hard practice will give the rider the independent position that is so necessary to success.

THE AIDS

$\mathcal{A}$S we've learned, the static dressage position is defined by two lines. There is a vertical line from your ear, to your shoulder, through your hip, to your heel. There is a second line drawn from your elbow to the horse's mouth. Once this static position is achieved, you must be able to maintain this position at all times. Once you have become, in effect, the perfect passenger, you must then learn to combine the perfect position with an ability to follow the horse's motion by use of balance alone. You then apply your aids without disturbing either the framework of your position or the following of the horse's paces and movements.

LEG AIDS

*N*OTICE that I have placed the leg aids first, before all other aids at the rider's disposal. The presence or absence of free forward motion dictates success or failure in most of a rider's work on horseback, and motion is produced by the legs, not the reins. There are three leg effects that are available to the rider.

1. The first leg effect is both legs at the girth. This is the most basic of all aids and will produce forward motion. The weight sinks slightly in the ankle, the knee softens, and both heels close at the girth. The hand must soften in order to allow the horse to go forward and straight. As the horse moves forward, maintain a supple arch in the small of your back, so as not to fall behind the motion or, inadvertently, pull on the reins.

2. The second leg effect is one leg at the girth. This leg is used either for bending, impulsion, or displacing the shoulders. Be sure to maintain the placement of this aid. It is quite common for riders to grip backward when applying the second leg effect. When instructors tell you to keep your horse between your inside leg and your outside rein, this is the leg aid they are looking for.

3. The third leg effect is one leg behind the girth. This leg is used to control or displace the haunches. Do not allow your upper body to slump forward and to the inside when using the third leg effect.

Any of these three aids may be combined. There is a false (fourth) leg position that you must avoid. The false effect consists of raising both heels, gripping back into the horse's sides, leaning forward, and pulling on the reins. This causes the horse to fall on his shoulders and go faster, but not to truly go forward. Don't mistake an increase in speed for an increase in impulsion.

Remember that impulsion comes from your legs. Your ability

to drive the horse forward with your seat bones is extremely limited. As an experiment, in the saddle, try this: halt; drop your reins and stirrups; and lift both legs away from the horse's sides. Now, without touching the horse's mouth or sides, try and "drive" the horse forward. You won't go far.

It takes years of repetition for a horse to associate seat-bone pressure with the leg aids. In the meantime, use your legs.

HAND AIDS

*T*HE following description of the five rein effects owes much to Colonel Harry D. Chamberlin's book *Riding and Schooling Horses,* published in 1934. While I make apologies to him, I would point out that I found his sketches in the *Manual of Equitation for the French Army,* which was published in 1912.

There are five rein effects. They are as follows:

1. *The open or leading rein.* This is a turning rein and is used to change direction. The hand is brought laterally away from the horse's withers in order to displace the head and neck to that side. The rider must take care not to lower or raise the hand that is opening the rein. The contact, in addition, should remain the same. Do not "float" the rein to the horse or combine open rein with direct rein. This will cause the neck to bend into a false position.

2. *The direct rein.* This rein is used to control direction and/or speed. The rider must be sure that the direct rein does not seek more from the horse than the horse can produce. The horse must be allowed to work in a frame where it can sustain self-carriage. The sensation is that of squeezing water from a sponge, not pulling on a rope. The hand should soften, squeeze, then soften again.

Think again about the way that the rider uses the reins to shorten the horse. The direct rein itself does not shorten the horse's stride as we require in dressage. What happens is that, if you pull backward on the reins as you apply the direct rein, you will shorten the neck but you will not shorten the stride. The horse truly shortens his stride when you "squeeze a sponge into

*W*HEN I say this is a "picture-perfect" position, that is not a compliment. You can have a vertical line ear-shoulder-hip-heel, and a straight line from your elbow to the bit, yet still not be able to ride. The purpose of a good position is to influence your horse. Because your horse is in motion, your position must be supple and elastic, not posed and rigid. The author on Miss Shannon Brooks's General Lion, Fox Covert Farm, Upperville, Virginia, 1993. BRANT GAMMA

the reins," then ask the horse to engage and shorten his step by using your seat and legs. We shorten the stride by closing the door, not by pulling the doorjamb back into our lap.

3. *The neck, or bearing, rein.* This rein supports the open leading rein by pressing against the horse's neck, and causes a change of direction to the opposite side. However, the hand applying the neck or bearing rein should never cross an invisible, perpendicular line drawn up from the center of the withers. The neck or bearing rein is usually applied with an open leading rein. Make sure that the contact while applying a neck rein does not intensify. This produces an indirect effect rather than the desired effect.

4. *The indirect rein in front of the withers.* This rein affects the horse from the withers forward. It is especially useful in straightening a horse that has learned to tip its head and hang on one rein, as in work at the half-pass. This rein is applied by drawing the hand back toward the rider's opposite shoulder, and acting across the withers. This achieves a pulley or lever effect against the horse's neck. The indirect rein in front of the withers should not be applied for a long period of time, but only as long as one foot of the horse is on the ground.

5. *The indirect rein behind the withers.* This rein acts across the horse's body in a diagonal fashion. The rider should draw his hand back toward his opposite hip. This bends the horse away from the direction of motion, and causes a shifting of his weight back to the opposite hip. It is mainly used as a turning rein and acts on the body of the horse as well as the neck. It is quite a powerful aid and should be used with care.

If the first three rein effects are applied consistently and with sensitivity, the rider will rarely need the indirect reins to correct the horse. Because the indirect reins block the action of the shoulder, they are very effective in bending the spine of the horse, but they also cause the horse to lose his forward movement. Anything that causes loss of motion must be viewed with great suspicion by the event rider.

I sometimes explain the use of the reins to the rider by using the following analogy: Imagine that you have a wheelbarrow full of manure, and you must take it downhill to dump it. As you push it over the crest of the hill the wheelbarrow is going to tend to gain speed. Naturally, you will lean back, pull against the handles, and set your heels; and this will help you keep the wheelbarrow balanced and under control until you get down to the muck pile. Dump the wheelbarrow in the pile. Now push the empty wheelbarrow back up the hill, turn it around at the crest of the hill, and park it.

Now get in the wheelbarrow. Kneel down, gripping the rim, then lean forward over your knees and nudge the wheelbarrow until it starts to roll down the hill. Obviously, with your weight in the front of the wheelbarrow, it is going to gain speed. Pull on the rim. Pull harder. Lean backward and pull. Scream, if it will make you feel better. Obviously, nothing is going to happen, except more speed.

Now, relax your hands on the rim of the wheelbarrow, remain kneeling, and shift your hips slightly back toward the handles of the wheelbarrow. This will cause the skids of the wheelbarrow to catch on the ground. By changing the balance of the wheelbarrow, you will be able to slow the wheelbarrow down without pulling on the rim. Use the reins the same way. If you can slow a wheelbarrow down by changing where you sit, you can slow a horse down without pulling on the reins.

We seek to ride our horse in "horizontal" balance, i.e., with a horizontal line from the mouth, to the point of rotation in the shoulder, to the hip. The horse that works freely and in an obedient fashion in this framework should score well at the international level.

One of my favorite means for making the rider aware of the use of the hands and reins is quite simple. Take a dressage whip, or a thin wooden dowel rod approximately 30 inches long, adjust the reins normally, and place the stick over the top of the hands, holding it lightly between the thumbs and forefingers. Now ride the horse normally in dressage. You'll be surprised at how much the stick moves.

Concentrate on keeping the stick level and quiet, both on straight lines and in the turns. When turning, the outside part of the stick goes forward as the inside hand comes back. This makes you follow correctly with the outside rein. As you come out of the turn and go into the straightaway, the outside end of the stick comes back and again remains still and perpendicular to the horse's withers.

Special care should be taken that the stick remains quiet when posting. Many times riders have a corkscrew motion in their posting trot. The stick will quickly point this out to you, and you will see the ends of the stick going in circles, up and down, one after the other. Another item to note is that when you go through corners and circles, you should not drop your inside hand, causing the inside end of the stick to point down toward the ground. The stick should remain horizontal at all times, and not show any excess motion. Easy to say, hard to do! Try it.

FURTHER AIDS

*T*HERE are other aids besides legs and reins that the rider has at his disposal, and we should examine them:

1. *The voice.* Probably the most powerful influence that you can have on the horse is the use of your voice, especially when employed in calm, soothing tones. Horses that have jumped too deep into a combination or horses that are starting to get excited in their dressage work can usually be affected by use of the voice. Stop work for a moment, and reward your horse, using a soft, crooning sort of voice. The horse will quickly associate the voice with relaxation.

A quiet "cluck" can help a horse go forward without disturbing him. But the horse will have to be taught to associate the noise of the cluck with the use of the leg, spurs, and/or whip. This association is very quickly formed and is a powerful aid when used under competitive circumstances.

2. *The seat bones.* Your seat bones are an extremely effective tool of communication since the horse is so sensitive to changes of your balance. However, much of our theory is incorrect when it speaks of the rider "driving" with his seat bones. The ability of the rider to force the horse forward with his seat bones is nonexistent.

The seat bones should rather be used as leading aids and not as a means of compulsion. For example, in the lateral work, placing your influence on the seat bone in the direction of motion will improve the horse's willingness to go forward.

THE World Championships is not the place to practice your technique. It's the place to use it to compete. Notice my inside leg and inside indirect rein while my back is turned to the judge. Carawich had a tendency to pop his shoulder in the medium trot on the circle, and I am correcting that while I can. The author on Carawich, World Championships, Lexington, 1978.   KARL LECK

Especially with Thoroughbreds, ride with the legs first, then the seat bones. The seat bones are a means of suggestion and indication, but they are not a means of compulsion.

3. *Spurs.* Spurs strengthen the effect of the leg. They can be used as a tool for punishment, but only under very limited circumstances and for a very short duration of time. Two or three sharp prods with the spur should be sufficient punishment for the horse. You must then find a way to get the horse to do what you want it to do without further resistance. Occasionally, horses will kick out or freeze when you use the spurs. This is a form of resistance and it must be met by a sharp reapplication of the leg and spur and, if necessary, support by the whip in order to send the horse forward. The horse must believe that God is on his back and the devil is at his belly.

4. *The whip.* There are two types of whips used in the mounted training of the horse. The short, jumping stick should be carried at all times by the rider when jumping. I have ridden horses that were so sensitive and hot that I did not wear spurs on them in the competition ring, but I always carried a whip. I never wanted to be in the position of the fellow who had brought a knife to a gunfight. Make sure that you have the ability to punish the horse if need be.

The second type of whip is a long dressage whip, which is used to help maintain the horse's impulsion and to increase his hindquarter response to the driving and bending aids of the rider. This aid can be used either to supplement your leg aids or, by reaching further back and touching the horse's hind quarters, to straighten or displace the quarters.

All of these aids should be used judiciously and with the idea in mind that when the horse needs a correction it was a mistake on the part of the rider that caused all of the trouble in the first place. For example, if you kick like the devil in front of a fence but fall backward on the reins in the air, you're probably going to get a refusal from the horse. After a short reminder to the horse with whip and spurs, go to the same jump again without taking back and maintain a consistent, light contact in the air. Most of the time you'll find the horse quite willing to jump as long as he is not confused by conflicting aids or overfaced. Note that I use a show-jumping example in the dressage section to make the point that all three disciplines are interrelated.

POSITION OF THE AIDS

*E*SPECIALLY on circles but throughout any bending exercise both your legs and reins have specific tasks. On a circle, your inside leg remains at the girth in the first leg effect. This provides impulsion and bends the horse's body. On the circle, your outside leg should be drawn back approximately 6 inches. This is the third leg effect and it will provide control and bending of the hind-quarters while remaining on the circle.

The inside rein should be in vibrant contact with the mouth. This is the direct rein and it controls the direction and flexion. The outside rein is used also in a direct fashion and controls the speed. Whenever you wish to slow, first soften your legs, engage your back, and squeeze the outside rein as if you were squeezing water out of a sponge. Work to perfect this technique so that your horse comes together from behind rather than by having his neck collapsed back into his shoulders.

The influence of your seat bones in the circle should be limited to a slight pressure upon the inside seat bone. If you have a bad habit, you can change the bad habit by exaggerating the reverse. What do I mean by this? It's simple. If you know that you round your shoulders forward over the horse's inside shoulder on turns and circles, then try and sit over the outside seat bone and have an exaggerated effect on the horse's outside hip.

Many times you can break through an old bad habit and get to a new level in your riding if you can exaggerate and demonstrate the opposite bad habit. The reason for this is that as you change from one extreme to the other, you will pass through the correct position. Do this enough times and the correct position will start to feel natural.

If you lean too far forward, practice leaning too far back. If you drop the horse in jumping at the point of takeoff, think to yourself that you should pull backward at the point of takeoff, and so on. You will be surprised at the progress you can make in training the horse and yourself when you break through old bad habits. Remember, practice does not make perfect. Perfect practice makes perfect.

THE THREE PACES

THE WALK

*T*HE first stage of riding is to understand the frameworks containing your position. The second stage of riding is sustaining this position while in motion. To do this you must understand the sensations produced by the horse's gaits. For example, at the walk you should feel a slight diagonal swaying motion in your seat bones. You should get the sensation that, as the left shoulder of the horse swings forward at the walk, your right seat bone is pushing down and diagonally left, and your right leg is closing at the girth in harmony with this motion. The walk will produce four beats.

The intensity of the leg aid is determined by the impulsion and length of stride that you require at that particular moment. The same feeling will occur on the other side. Thus, you feel that, while sitting perfectly still in your shoulders and upper body, you follow the oscillation of the horse's back with your hips and seat bones.

The rider must attempt to maintain contact throughout the four beats of the walk if the walk is going to be free and easy. The elbows and hands should move back and forth in rhythm with the horse's step. While the motion is slight, failing to follow this motion correctly is one of the chief reasons for the poor quality of the walk that is shown during most dressage tests.

The horse's mouth is a much more sensitive instrument than most riders realize. Even the slightest interruption of contact causes the horse to become irregular and shorten his step.

The following action will also be important in the show jumping and cross-country phases. The show jumping rider must be able to sit in perfect balance while a horse jumps underneath him, allowing full use of the horse's head and neck while maintaining an unchanging tension of the reins.

The cross-country rider must quietly support the galloping horse with the reins throughout the four beats of the gallop, especially if the horse becomes tired. He must be able to sit well behind the motion, yet slip the reins as the horse requires, never restricting, never losing the motion of the head and neck as felt through the reins.

Whichever discipline we are competing in, we should strive to keep our horse perfectly balanced between our legs and our hands at all times.

THE CANTER

*T*HE walk is the easiest of the three paces for you to sit and be comfortable, while the canter is the next easiest. The reason for this is the easy swinging motion that a calm horse produces. The sensation you should have is that your inside seat bone is slightly in advance of your outside seat bone. The horse advances the muscles along the inside of its body in order to produce the lead and you should follow this.

Whenever I discuss pressure on one seat bone I'm referring to a very slight influence. Do not displace the upper body or twist the shoulders. A swinging motion in the three-beat canter should be felt from the small of your back into the seat. Your upper body and arms should remain still.

What we describe as "still" is actually something quite different. You are remaining attached to a horse cantering anywhere from 8 to 15 miles an hour. What actually happens is that you remain "still" in relation to the horse, while the horse is in motion. So that, for example, the distance between the back of the elbow and the horse's mouth remains the same.

At the canter you should feel that you are sitting on a playground swing. Your back should sway back and forth in rhythm with the stride. One of the most common bad habits in dressage riding is to "post" at the canter. The cause of this is that while the rider swings his hips forward in rhythm with the first beat of the

A GOOD position at the canter. Because Anne's back is supple, she will maintain contact with the horse's back during the three beats of the canter. Horses tend to go the way that we ride them. When you have a position like this, good things are going to happen. Fox Covert Farm, Upperville, Virginia, 1993. BRANT GAMMA

canter, he then fixes his back and hips, and subsequently is pushed or "posts" out of the saddle. He returns to the saddle at the third beat, swings his back and hips forward, and repeats. This causes a false posting motion. When seated in the saddle you need constant, rather than intermittent, contact with the horse's back.

The playground swing analogy will help you because it causes you not only to swing forward with your hips but to draw them back again. This should be done without disturbing the position of your upper body, arms, or hands. The advancement of the inside seat bone does not mean that your weight shifts to the inside. In fact, many times you will feel the horse in better balance if you sit over the inside seat bone but lean over your hip on the horse's outside.

Riders and trainers often put too much emphasis on driving the inside leg of the horse farther under the body at the canter. This is not efficient because at that point the horse's pace is one quarter of the way through the cycle of the three-beat canter and the period of suspension. You can quickly improve the canter if the emphasis is placed more upon the outside hind leg of the horse. By causing the first beat of the canter to be placed farther under the horse's body, the next two beats of the canter will correspondingly reach farther forward, thus achieving the desired effect.

THE TROT

*T*HE trot is the most difficult of the three paces for the rider to follow. The reason for this is that the motion is not just up and down, but also side to side. Longe a horse without side reins and observe carefully the motion of the horse's pelvis. When the horse trots, you will see that the points of the hips rise and fall in rhythm with the steps.

For example, as the horse pushes back with his right hind leg the left hip comes up. This produces a lifting and twisting motion under the saddle. Alternately, when the horse brings his right hind leg under the body, his hip sinks on the left side.

Failure to follow this motion is the major cause of bouncing at the trot. You can correct this by the following exercise: look down your nose at the horse's shoulders and observe the sequence of the front footfalls. As the right front foot of the horse strikes the ground, push forward and down with your right seat bone. Alternatively, as the left front foot of the horse strikes the ground, push forward and down with the left seat bone.

This exercise will not work until you relax and produce a lateral, swaying motion in your back. This motion is not measured in inches but in fractions of inches. Your upper body must remain poised and still throughout the exercise. It is common to see riders swinging their shoulders, vainly seeking the following action of the seat bones, yet maintaining a rigid hip and lower back connection with the horse, and continuing to bounce.

If you attempt this exercise and it does not produce a more fluid and soft sensation, try again. This time stand slightly from one stirrup to the other. Put a slight amount of pressure down in each heel in rhythm with the trot. As the horse's right front foot strikes the ground, your right heel should sink slightly. As the horse's left front foot strikes the ground, your left heel should sink. This exercise will help to produce the required sensation. It is quite common to produce an exaggerated motion at first. But this motion should be small and invisible. As soon as you become supple in your back the horse's step will improve markedly. Practice this exercise until the onlooker can see no extra motion in your arms or shoulders.

DRESSAGE TRAINING

*T*HE majority of your training will be in dressage. There are three different places you should train your horse: a dressage arena, a large riding ring, and a large field (hopefully with undulating terrain). Whatever the location you choose, you should not exceed forty-five minutes of dressage exercise daily.

The dressage arena is the place to work on the movements of your dressage test, to practice transitions called for by your test, and to improve your accuracy. Do not practice the entire dressage test often, as your horse will quickly start to anticipate the movements. Too much work in the arena will make your horse stale and cause him to lose impulsion.

You can do all the movements and transitions required by your test in a large ring without the danger of boredom and loss of impulsion. Analyze the movements that give your horse difficulty and develop exercises to improve those movements. For example, a horse that rushes after his extended trot should be taught extended trot, halt, rein-back, working trot, and so on. Training a three-day event horse is a series of compromises. The large ring is a good compromise between the compression of an arena and the possible hard ground of a large field.

Before beginning outdoor exercise you must ensure that the footing is suitable. Field dressage, i.e., working over undulating terrain while practicing dressage movements, is an excellent form of exercise and training. If you cannot make a dent in the ground by digging in with your heel, however, then the ground is too hard for extended work and you should do your training in an arena with prepared footing. Field dressage prevents the horse from becoming ring-sour; helps prepare the horse for the Roads and Tracks; and, most important, helps break up resistance in the horse's topline.

AT first glance, this looks like a lovely photo. Look again. The horse's mouth tells you what is really going on here. Karen and Bill (The Optimist) are in the dressage arena for the Olympics, and Bill is pulling like a train. Karen is solving this by taking the weight of the reins into an arched back and sinking into her heels to hold the horse together. If she had raised her hands and pulled back against the horse, she would have been in trouble. Ride your horse with your seat and legs, not your reins. Karen Lende on Mr. and Mrs. Bertram Firestone's The Optimist, Olympics, Seoul, 1988.   KARL LECK

Working over undulating terrain, practicing lengthenings uphill, practicing collections downhill, doing a medium walk on the bit while going down a steep hill, lateral work across slight inclines—all are useful. The horse finds it difficult to resist when his topline is continually changing attitude and shape. Ride with your stirrups one hole shorter than your normal dressage length and allow the horse to carry his head and neck in a slightly lower position than his competitive level would otherwise require. "Long and low" and "showing your horse the way to the ground" describe a classical training method that can be utilized either in the dressage arena or over undulating terrain. Use this technique to relax and engage your horse by teaching him to step from your inside leg to your outside rein. The withers should be the high point of the horse's body, the nose the most forward point, and the paces should remain regular and unhurried. At no time should the plane of the horse's face be behind the vertical. There is a current fad that forces horses to work in an overflexed position. Ignore the fad and concentrate on working your horse calmly and classically.

Whether you are working long and low or on the bit, in an arena or out in the field, practice all the dressage movements for your level every day. Regardless of your location, you should use the following basic movements on a daily basis. The trained horse should practice halt, rein-back, turn on the forehand, turn on the haunches, leg-yielding, shoulder-in, haunches-in, two-track, counter-canter, and extensions and collections at all three paces.

THE HALT

$\mathcal{I}$T is amazing how many riders will struggle endlessly around a dressage arena on a horse that knows how to halt, complaining bitterly of the horse's pulling and leaning against the bit. Yet they will not use, to its best advantage, the simplest of all movements—the halt.

Most horses can be persuaded to stop their forward motion, after a greater or lesser struggle. You must develop your ability to use the reins in a resisting fashion without pulling backward. The reins are sponges, not ropes. Do not "drive" a horse into the halt; "support" the horse into the halt. If you close your legs too aggressively, you will cause the horse to lean on the reins rather than to retard his motion.

The mental image that you should carry is one in which you are attempting to slow the horse's motion, not to shorten his neck. Various exercises, such as carrying a riding whip balanced over the thumbs or holding a neck strap under the little finger, will ensure that your hand does not act backward as you ask for the halt. At first, you should be satisfied with a halt that takes quite a few steps to develop but then is produced in a calm, balanced fashion.

The use of the voice can be quite beneficial at the early stages of training as an artificial aid. For example, riding the horse directly at the wall of the arena and then using the voice alone will many times produce quite an attractive halt. Once the horse begins to associate the voice aid with halting and then reward, you can start to move the halt farther and farther back from the wall, at the same time teaching the horse to associate the voice with the back and rein aids.

The rider should not confuse a quiet halt, where the hands quietly resist the forward motion, the lower leg softens, and the muscles of the rider's lower back resist, with a savage jerking of the horse's mouth. This causes the horse to stop on his forehand, mouth open with pain. The first example is training and will produce a better horse. The second example is cruelty and will do nothing except ingrain the horse's and rider's bad habits.

Once the horse can halt attractively, you are ready to start work off the rail. Introduce the horse to the concept of walking and trotting on the center line of the arena without taking advantage of the balancing effect of the wall.

Because of the importance of a first impression on the dressage judge, you should practice work on the center line and quarter lines regardless of the state of training of your horse. At the highest stages of training, the horse should be quite comfortable doing linked transitions between trot and canter, walk and trot, walk and canter, canter and walk, and so on, on the center line without deviating with his quarters, losing the stability of his head and neck, or losing the rhythm of his paces.

THE REIN-BACK

THE rein-back is another powerful training tool. In a fashion similar to the halt, you must learn to ask the horse to back by closing the fingers but not pulling backward. Your fingers close first, then your legs close at the girth. Do not displace your body backward or forward in asking the horse to back. If the horse shows signs of resistance, you can resort to the use of the voice. If the horse continues to resist, probably the best thing for you to do is to have a trainer on the ground tap the horse softly on the foreleg with a long dressage whip while you reestablish the aids for the rein-back, especially the voice. The horse will soon associate the aids with the motion and will step backward quietly without compulsion. The trainer should then move away until, finally, you and your horse can produce the rein-back on your own.

This movement should not be practiced to excess, as it will make your horse restive at the halt during a dressage test. The horse should always be asked for a few steps more than the test requires. This will keep your horse from anticipating and moving out of the rein-back too soon. The halt and the rein-back both displace the weight of the horse behind the saddle and, thus, have a very effective part in the daily training of the event horse.

Done correctly, these schooling movements will balance the horse, and you will discover that you did not need all those "gadget" bits after all.

THE TURN ON THE FOREHAND

THE turn on the forehand is an easy movement to teach the horse. It will become the basis for many of the later, more sophisticated movements. The aids for the turn on the forehand are simple. With the horse at the halt, parallel to the track, place your outside leg behind the girth and open the outside rein slightly. Ask the horse to displace his haunches to the inside by pressure from your outside leg.

Your horse should describe a half-circle with his haunches, leaving his inside foreleg in the same place. The outside hind leg of your horse should cross in front of the inside hind leg. No emphasis should be placed on the bending of the horse's head and neck. Indeed, you should attempt to keep the horse's spine straight during this movement, seeking only enough bending to see the eyelashes of the inside eye (inside relative to the horse's bending, not relative to the ring). Use the legs rather than the reins to produce the movement.

The turn on the forehand is an excellent means of getting a young horse to accept your leg and engage, rather than jumping forward when you make contact with your leg on his side.

The two most common mistakes that your horse will make in the turn on the forehand will be either to move forward or to step backward. The turn on the forehand is an exercise of the combination and balancing of aids. Therefore, should the horse step forward during the turn on the forehand, it is because your horse has overreacted to the use of the leg. Soften the driving leg, without removing it entirely, and retard the forward motion by using the rein opposite your active leg. Alternatively, if your horse steps back from the turn on the forehand, you have used too much rein. Soften your hands and close your leg.

Riders tend to overanalyze this sort of mistake by the horse. It is really quite simple: if the horse moves off the pivot foot, analyze what aid has produced the mistake, soften that aid, and emphasize the other aid until the equilibrium of the horse has been reestablished. It is most important to soften the original aid. This will make the alternate aid feel stronger to the horse without changing the intensity of the second aid.

THE TURN ON THE HAUNCHES

THE turn on the haunches is a more advanced movement. While the turn on the forehand lowers the horse in front and supples the hindquarters, the turn on the haunches engages the hindquarters of the horse, supples the shoulders, and elevates the forehand.

In order to produce a turn on the haunches, halt your horse parallel to the wall; open the inside rein and produce a slight bending to the inside. Bring the outside rein into a neck rein or bearing rein position. Your inside leg stays at the girth; your outside leg is displaced slightly behind the girth to maintain an inside bending and to displace the shoulders. The horse should pivot to the inside around his inside hind leg, with the inside hind foot remaining on the same spot. The outside legs of your horse should cross in front of the inside and he should pivot around the inside hind leg with his shoulders.

Again, the mistakes that the horse can make are quite simple. If he steps forward off the pivot leg, soften your inside leg and, if necessary, resist with the outside rein. This rein should act in a straight line back toward the rider's outside hip and should not be used as an indirect rein of opposition across the withers. If necessary, your outside rein can become stronger.

If the horse falls back from the closing effect of your hands, soften the reins, allow the horse to step forward a few paces, halt, and then resume the movement. If your horse is very green, it is quite allowable for him to describe a small forward half-circle with his hindquarters in order to make sure that he does not fall behind the bit.

LATERAL MOVEMENTS

*T*HE lateral movements consist of leg-yielding, shoulder-in, haunches-in, and two-track. They should be taught to the horse in this sequence. They are powerful tools to prevent the horse from rushing, and to promote leg response and lateral suppleness.

Every dressage movement has both good things and bad things about it. For example, the halt and rein-back are effective means for preventing the horse from rushing in his dressage work. However, as we've seen, too much of this can cause a horse to become restive and unsteady at the halt, and behind the bit in the rein-back.

While lateral work increases the leg response of the horse and the suppleness of the hindquarters, it can also cause the horse to lose impulsion. You must become a bit of a juggler in the movements that you ask the horse to perform. After a period of work on leg-

*W*HEN you go in the dressage arena, you go in to compete. Put your eyes on the next letter, plan your transitions, and ride toward that point. Lower legs could be closer, hands lower, weight a little farther back over the outside seat bone. The author on Mr. and Mrs. Richard Thompson's Castlewellan, Rolex Kentucky, 1983.   BOB STRAUS

I ASKED Shannon to show me what happens when a horse is pulled rather than pushed into a leg-yielding. I call this position "neck-yielding" rather than leg-yielding. Shannon Brooks on General Lion, Fox Covert Farm, Upperville, Virginia, 1993. BRANT GAMMA

yielding and shoulder-in, he should be in an engaged, balanced frame. The horse should now be asked to produce an attractive lengthening of the stride or extension, depending on his state of training.

Alternatively, too much lengthening of the stride or extension can tend to make your horse rush, and it is exactly this sort of frame that will be most improved by a sequence of lateral work. Too much emphasis on any one movement can actually produce incorrect results, whereas a judicious mixture of training movements will improve your horse rapidly.

I mentioned earlier that the lateral movements should be taught in this sequence: leg-yielding, shoulder-in, haunches-in, and two-track. This is done because each movement presupposes knowledge of preceding work. The leg-yielding and shoulder-in are produced with the bending going away from the direction of motion. Haunches-in and two-track are produced with the bending going into the direction of motion, and thus are more difficult for the horse.

LEG-YIELDING

*L*EG-YIELDING should be taught to the horse first at the walk along the wall. I use the wall a great deal in the dressage training of the horse because it allows me to substitute an outside influence for the restraining function of the reins. The rider should attempt to keep the reins as light as possible at all times. (Once you get a horse three-day event fit, you will rarely have difficulty getting him to take a firm contact of the reins.)

By teaching leg-yielding along the wall you can avoid using much rein to produce the movement. Displacing your outside leg should be sufficient to bring the hindquarters in off the wall. The horse should proceed with his shoulders on the track at a 30-degree angle to the wall. The bending of his body should be only enough to allow the rider to see the eyelashes of the horse's outside eye (outside relative to the ring, not to the horse's bending).

Many times a better leg-yielding is produced when you attempt to keep the horse straight. The main aid, indeed almost the only aid, is the outside leg behind the girth (again, outside the ring). This is the third leg effect referred to earlier in this chapter.

You should produce four separate and distinct tracks with the horse's legs. The onlooker standing in the track at the far corner should see each individual leg as the horse proceeds along the track in leg-yielding.

It is quite common for horses to wander back and forth from not enough angle to too much angle. When the horse wanders and evades your leg, change the placement of the outside leg. For example, if the horse resists and attempts to bring his hip back to the wall, displace your leg farther to the rear rather than increasing the intensity of the leg aid. Alternatively, some horses will get the idea of what it is that the rider's asking and will become overly sensitive with their hindquarters. These horses will attempt to produce a 45- or even a 90-degree angle to the wall.

Rather than trying to correct this with a combination of other aids, first soften the driving leg and bring it farther forward to the girth. This acts more on the shoulders than on the hindquarters, and should be sufficient to reestablish the required angle. If this does not completely solve the problem, however, use of the opposite rein will usually produce the required angle.

A very good exercise is to produce the leg-yielding at the walk with the reins in one hand (the hand opposite the active leg). This serves as an excellent test of whether you are producing the movement from your leg or from your reins.

Another exercise is to be able to break the rein contact, especially with the outside rein (outside the ring), during the leg-yielding. This ensures that your horse is stepping laterally from your active leg to your opposite hand. Whatever bend exists in your horse's body should exist because it has been produced by your leg and not because it has been compelled by your hand.

Throughout the work in leg-yielding, and indeed in all lateral work, you should maintain a slight influence with the seat bone in the direction of motion. You should experiment with this in order to ascertain the best balance for each particular horse. However, it is a very rare animal, usually warm-blooded rather than Thoroughbred, that requires you to sit above the driving leg. Attempt to lead the motion with your seat bone rather than to sit behind the motion. This is true of all four lateral movements.

Once leg-yielding has been introduced at the walk along the rail, the horse can then be taught leg-yielding at the walk on the

*W*HAT strikes me more than anything else about this photograph is the economy of aids required to produce a lateral movement. The leg-yielding here is produced solely by the active, left leg. The rest of the aids are very quiet, allowing the horse to move freely forward to the side. Eyes up, Jim. The author on Miss Shannon Brooks's General Lion, Fox Covert Farm, Upperville, Virginia, 1993.   BRANT GAMMA

diagonal, leg-yielding at the trot, and leg-yielding on a circle. The work in leg-yielding should be viewed as both a movement in itself and, when done as leg-yielding to the inside, as a preparatory phase of the shoulder-in.

SHOULDER-IN

A GREAT deal of resistance by the horse can be avoided if you start work on shoulder-in by first producing an inside leg-yielding. Then bring your horse's shoulders back toward the track by bringing your active leg forward to the girth. The shoulder-in produces three tracks when the horse moves parallel to the wall. The onlooker standing in the corner should see the outside hind leg on one track, the inside hind leg and the outside foreleg on the second track, and the inside foreleg as a third track coming directly toward him. The points of the horse's hip should remain perpendicular to the wall.

This is an excellent movement to supple your horse's shoulders and engage his hindquarters. It also improves your ability to coordinate your aids, especially to put your horse between your inside leg and outside hand.

The aids for the shoulder-in are as follows: the inside leg is active at the girth, the outside leg is placed behind the girth to prevent your horse from "climbing the wall" with his outside hind leg, the inside rein opens slightly and leads the forehand off the track, and the outside rein controls the speed and displaces the shoulders in off the track by a slight bearing action. The rider's weight should be placed slightly over the leading seat bone. The emphasis here must remain on the horse's forward movement and not on the bending or angle.

If your horse resists coming off the wall in the shoulder-in, put him into inside leg-yielding first in order to produce an angle to the wall. Then bring the shoulders back over in front of the hindquarters until they are aligned on three tracks rather than on four. The hardest part of the shoulder-in is to make sure that the hindquarters remain perpendicular to the wall even as the bend in front of the saddle begins to increase.

The bending of the shoulder-in should be sufficient to allow the rider to see the eyelashes of the horse's inside eye. Horses that hang on the wall with their shoulders should be placed in an inside leg-yielding position first and then brought back to shoulder-in. Horses that run from the inside leg must be restrained by the outside hand. The outside hand acts directly back toward your outside hip, not across the withers.

The most common mistake in shoulder-in is in the action of the inside rein. The inside rein should be away from the inside neck of the horse. Your horse should be suspended between your inside leg and outside hand. If the horse is correctly balanced, you will have the feeling that, at any time, you can ease the contact with the inside rein for one step and then regain a light following contact without having the horse change either his direction, speed, balance, or flexion. While the leg-yielding can be performed only at the walk and the trot, the shoulder-in can be performed at all three paces.

The first two lateral movements, leg-yielding and shoulder-in, are taught to the horse with a bending away from the direction of motion. The next two lateral movements, haunches-in and two-track, are taught with the horse's body bent into the direction of motion. This accounts for the movements' increasing difficulty and the increasing sophistication required from the rider.

HAUNCHES-IN

*H*AUNCHES-IN should be viewed as two-track along the wall. It is an excellent exercise for collecting the horse and overcoming resistance of the hindquarters. Your outside leg is the dominant aid; it brings the quarters in off the track. At the same time, your inside rein suggests enough bend so that you can see the inside eye of the horse. The inside leg creates the impulsion, and the outside rein controls the speed and the shoulders. As always, your weight is on the seat bone in the direction of motion.

The advantage of haunches-in is that you have the wall in front of you in order to keep your horse from running from your leg, just as earlier in leg-yielding. Therefore, the reins will remain soft and light, and you can concentrate on forward motion and correct bending. As your horse proceeds down the wall in haunches-in, an onlooker standing in the far corner should see three distinct tracks. The outside foreleg is on the track, the inside foreleg and the outside hind leg form the second track, and the inside hind leg forms the third track. The points of the ears are perpendicular to the wall. The outside foreleg and the outside hind leg should cross in front of the inside legs, and you should, at all times, be able to drop the contact with the inside rein for a step. This ensures that the horse is still balanced between your inside leg and outside hand.

THE TWO-TRACK

*T*HE final lateral movement taught to horses is the two-track. The two-track is a diagonal movement, and, like the shoulder-in and the haunches-in, can be performed at all three paces. The bending of the horse is greatest in front of the body. The points of the hip remain perpendicular to the wall, while the bending increases from the point of the croup forward through the horse's body. The shoulders must always be slightly in advance of the hindquarters, and the outside legs cross in front of the inside legs of the horse.

Your aids are: outside hind leg behind the girth to displace the horse's body laterally; inside leg to create and maintain impulsion; inside rein opening slightly to suggest the direction; and outside rein controlling the speed and the forehand of the horse. Your weight is on the leading seat bone. The emphasis here, as in all of the lateral movements, must be on forward motion, not bending.

Imagine a rope tied from the inside point of the horse's shoulder to an opposite point on the far wall. The rope is being pulled in so that the horse is drawn diagonally across the ring. This image will help to convince you to ride forward in the two-track rather than backward. It cannot be emphasized enough that the bending must be created by the legs and not by the hands, while the reins should stay soft and light. There should be nothing crablike, stiff, or mechanical about the movement. The horse should maintain his regularity and carriage and move energetically forward to the side.

In review, the four lateral movements are leg-yielding, shoulder-in, haunches-in, and two-track. Notice that the movements are taught to the horse in ascending order of difficulty, i.e., the haunches-in is more complex, and therefore more difficult, than the shoulder-in.

Any attempt that you can make to simplify rather than complicate your riding will prove beneficial to the horse. Whenever you run into resistance from your horse, you should first attempt to simplify whatever you are asking the horse to do. This usually means removing one or more extra aids rather than adding or intensifying aids to a horse that is already demonstrably confused.

It may help you to think of lateral movements in the following manner: Leg-yielding is produced solely by one aid. That aid is the outside leg behind the girth. Shoulder-in can be produced solely by two aids—the inside leg and the outside hand. Haunches-in can be produced by three aids—the inside leg at the girth, the outside leg behind the girth, and the outside rein. And finally, two-track (the most complex of the movements) requires all four aids—inside leg at the girth, outside leg behind the girth, inside rein to control the direction and the bending, and outside rein to control the speed.

COUNTER-CANTER

*C*OUNTER-CANTER is an excellent suppling exercise. In order for your horse to learn to hold his lead, introduce counter-canter gradually. For example, counter-canter work becomes easier outside the arena, as you are not forced by walls and fences to hold the horse on a turn of a certain size. By starting with very mild, sweeping serpentines back and forth from true canter to counter-canter, you can quickly improve the ability of the horse to sustain a particular lead, thereby making quicker progress and, incidentally, preventing the horse from doing a flying change.

Sit over the seat bone of the lead—for example, right seat bone for right lead. Maintain just enough bending into the lead to see the lashes of your horse's inside eye and keep the cadence the same as you ride through the curve.

CANTER CORRECTION

*B*ECAUSE so much of a three-day event is ridden at the canter and gallop, it is essential that you keep your horse straight and balanced.

*C*OUNTER-CANTER is an excellent suppling exercise. Here, I'm preparing to turn left while maintaining the right lead. I will keep the horse almost straight in front, put my weight on my right seat bone, and create the turn with my left leg. Then I will concentrate on making a smooth curve while keeping the rhythm. The author on Miss Shannon Brooks's General Lion, Fox Covert Farm, Upperville, Virginia, 1993. BRANT GAMMA

It is quite common for horses to canter with their hindquarters in off the track. This is a tricky evasion to deal with because it is one of the few times in classical riding that you cannot solve your problem by riding straight forward. If you ride forward more, you will cause your horse's inside hip to float off the wall more. If you attempt to correct it with your inside rein, the horse will collapse around your inside leg more. If you attempt to straighten the horse with your inside leg, many times the horse will do a flying change behind. So, what to do?

Think of the horse's canter in this fashion. When a horse is cantering perfectly straight, he forms two parallel lines between the bit, the points of his shoulders, and his hocks. These parallel lines proceed straight down the track. When the horse canters like a dog, he still has his mouth and his hocks in a straight line, but the shoulders have collapsed to the outside.

In order to prevent this, bring your outside leg forward until it is at the girth. Press, in rhythm with the stride, with your outside leg. At the same time soften the inside rein and apply neck or bearing rein with the outside rein. Do not attempt to have an effect on the bit or the hocks. Merely try to push the shoulders back from the outside until they realign with the mouth and the hocks. The horse will probably become straight. This condition will last for two or three strides before the horse will evade again by dropping its shoulder to the outside.

Reapply the aids and ride the horse quietly forward so long as he stays straight. As you reach the corner and take the horse back, make sure that you use the outside rein more than the inside rein in order to help control the outside shoulder.

It will take continued repetitions of this correction to make your horse truly straight at the canter. You will find that when you apply these corrective aids the horse will become straight but he will drift slightly in off the track. Don't worry about that yet. Ride the horse straight forward. When he collapses his shoulder to the outside, correct him and ride him straight forward again. You will sometimes wind up several horses' width in off the track by the time you reach the far corner. But at the same time, the major part of the work down the long side has been with the horse straight through his body, and that is what you are seeking. Once you can put the horse completely straight, it will be easy to ride him in the track that you desire.

As an aside, it is important that eventers are able to do a flying change at the canter. However, present international tests place a great emphasis on the counter-canter. Therefore, when you wish to perform a flying change, you should come up into a "two point," or jumping position, rather than a seated dressage position. You want to create the association in the horse's mind that, so long as you sit on his back, his lead should not change; then, as soon as you come up off the horse's back, it is allowable for him to produce his changes. This will become increasingly important as your dressage and show jumping work become more sophisticated.

RESISTANCE

*T*HE rider's independent position is crucial to prevention of resistance. If the rider's body is contorted in order to place one aid on the horse, the horse becomes so confused that he then begins to resist. Most resistance in horses is caused not by unwillingness on the horse's part but rather by misunderstanding due to aids that are too complex, too strong, or contradictory.

There are five basic reasons for resistance in the horse:

1. *Clashing or incorrect aids.* If you ask your horse to go forward with your legs but do not soften the reins, you are going to produce a response that many riders will interpret as resistance. However, if you make sure that you soften your reins as you close your legs, most horses are going to go forward. It's entirely possible that, rather than the horse being resistant, the rider has used incorrect aids on the horse.

If you do not understand the correct position of the aids for the two-track, it is going to be difficult to produce a correct response from the horse. Most problems in training horses can be solved if you will stop and think for a moment. Say to yourself, "What is it that a rider does wrong that will produce this sort of response from the horse?" Then, by changing the

*E*VEN though I'm trying to show you what happens when you collapse your hip, I'm not very happy about it. You can see that the horse's weight has transferred to his left shoulder. Next he will start a four-beat canter, and the chances are very good that he will then change or break. Looking down isn't going to help. The author on Miss Shannon Brooks's General Lion, Fox Covert Farm, Upperville, Virginia, 1993. BRANT GAMMA

position and application of your aids, you will quite often produce a much better result from the horse.

2. *Lack of understanding on the part of the horse.* Horses may resist, not through unwillingness, but through a lack of understanding. For example, a horse that has just been started and is capable of going at the walk, trot, and canter on a loose rein in large circles is going to be perplexed if we suddenly apply the aids for a flying change of lead every third stride.

Again, the horse may produce a response that we interpret as resistance, but it is not the horse that is wrong—it is the rider. You must make sure that your aids are correct and that you are asking the horse in a clear fashion for a movement that the horse has already been introduced to, or has been prepared for by simpler exercises.

3. *Inability of the horse.* By inability I mean that the horse is incapable of producing the movement either through being lame or through lack of preparation and physical condition. Horses that have just started in serious dressage work can rarely produce a correct extension. Their inability to do so should be viewed as the absence of training rather than the presence of resistance.

4. *Unwillingness of the horse.* Horses may be unwilling to attempt certain exercises or requests of the rider due to a repeated series of bad experiences on the part of the horse. For example, horses may sulk at their extensions, knowing full well that it is within their capabilities. But they are tired of carrying riders who throw themselves backward against the reins every time the horse extends. This can be dealt with, but the rider must analyze the reason for the resistance and develop a plan for the improvement of his own position rather than attacking the resistance directly.

5. *The horse is a rogue.* Probably the least common form of resistance is that of a horse that from birth willingly sets himself, mentally and physically, against the rider. Very few riders are skilled enough to deal with this sort of animal. My best advice to you is to sell this horse. Now.

I have dealt with only two or three horses in my lifetime that I thought were truly aggressive toward humans. Even with the best of intentions, horses can be dangerous creatures. So when they turn their faculties on you, with an eye toward defeating you rather than assisting you, it's time to get out. Fortunately, this is an exceedingly rare case. Most bad horses have been made bad by their riders.

Throughout your dressage work you must remain aware of the interplay of the three disciplines. For example, some horses will not be as good in their dressage on the day following a canter. These horses might be better off doing field dressage on the following day, then practicing some show jumping; and then, three days after the gallop, going into a dressage arena and practicing some movements. Other horses, of a more sluggish temperament, may be exactly the opposite. Some horses are affected in their dressage by the show jumping. You should be aware of your horse's reaction the day following a hard day's show jumping lesson. This will improve some horses and make their back feel more supple. It will make other horses more stiff, as they have had to use their back to an unusual degree on the day before.

It is essential that you adjust your schedule as you go along. It's no good saying that you are going to practice dressage movements today if your horse is sweating and galloping sideways as you leave the stables. You had better throw the schedule away for that day, concentrate on stabilizing the horse mentally, and then attempt to make some progress if you are able to do that. You must use the schedule to train the horse. Don't let the schedule train you.

I think that the interplay of the various phases is the most fascinating part of training three-day event horses and the one that requires the greatest horsemanship. Many riders can ride good dressage tests. A few riders can produce horses that are fit to run over big, long cross-country courses. And some riders have the ability to be exceedingly accurate in the approach to show jumps. But not many riders have the ability to combine all of these skills to produce a horse at the event that is perfectly balanced, both mentally and physically. That is the true challenge of three-day eventing.

5

Cross-Country

GENERAL COMMENTS

*T*HE three-day event rules are set up so that the emphasis is on your performance cross-country. This is not as true at the lower levels as at the higher but if you have a refusal or a fall cross-country, the chances are pretty good that you are not going to figure in the placings. So cross-country should be the strongest of your three skills. It should also be the one that you enjoy the most, with all its high speeds and greater risks. At some point in your development as a rider you're going to have to ask yourself, "Is this the sport for me?" Every rider has a different amount of nerve. Most riders have different levels of nerve on different horses. It's up to you to find out just exactly how far you really want to go in the sport—and how far you're willing to take your mount.

POSITION OF THE RIDER

*T*HE position of the cross-country rider is supremely important. In show jumping we only have to deal with fences on level ground, and we jump them at much slower speeds.

In addition, going cross-country we are jumping at all sorts of angles up, down, and across the terrain. The first rule of cross-country is that you don't win if you fall off. Be secure. Remember

*I*F you cut out the horse from this photo, Karen would still land on her feet. This is how you jump a big fence into deep water. The placement of her lower leg makes for the security of her upper body, and the reins are adjusted perfectly. She has lifted her hands slightly to maintain contact as Max begins his recovering stride. Karen Lende on Mr. Richard Thompson's Mr. Maxwell, Badminton, 1992.   BRANT GAMMA

*O*NE of my favorite pictures on one of my favorite horses. This is a good place to be in when things are going well and the horse is truly galloping and jumping over big fences—lower leg slightly in front, light steady contact, the weight behind the horse's shoulders, head and eyes up looking for the next jump. The author on Kilkenny, Badminton, 1968. MONTY

that it is possible to jump without stirrups, but it is impossible to jump without grip. So while an emphasis on weight in the ankles is necessary, the greatest emphasis should be on a strong position of the entire lower leg, supported by a positive feel of your knees in the saddle. The grip should be distributed equally from the inside point of the knee to the inside point of the ankle.

The feet should be placed farther into the stirrup than for show jumping. The ball of your foot should be in front of the tread of the stirrup, with your weight resting on, at least, the arch of your foot or, if it is more comfortable for you, with your foot all the way "home" in the stirrup. What you lose in flexibility you are going to gain in security. It is better to be safe than sensitive.

In show jumping we attempt to keep the stirrup leather perpendicular to the ground at all times so that our feet remain underneath our body. The stirrups substitute for the ground when we take off and land. This is not quite true of cross-country riding because the terrain changes. Here we have to concentrate on maintaining a stirrup leather which is vertical. This will provide a base of support for you as you either push your upper body forward going up slopes, or allow your upper body to get behind the stirrup, with the stirrup leather in front of the girth, when going down a slope or landing over drops.

Analysis of photos and slow motion videotapes will show you that most riders get into trouble after their foot and stirrup leather get in the wrong place. If the foot is in the correct place underneath you, you can catch your balance and survive situations that otherwise would put you on the ground.

You should be able to move easily back and forth from a two-point to a three-point position. By two-point, I mean that you are supporting your weight on the two points of your knees, with your seat above the saddle. By three-point, I mean that your seat is in the saddle, and your weight is resting on your two seat bones and your pubic bone. When I mention a light three-point, I want you to keep your shoulders in front of your hips even when seated in the saddle.

Because of the speed involved in going cross-country you should be in a two-point position, with the seat bones out of the saddle, while galloping between fences. This allows the horse's back to pass underneath you without being burdened by your weight. As the horse gallops, have the feeling that your knee flexes up and

ABOVE:

*A*LTHOUGH the horse has begun his takeoff motion, Karen will not leave the saddle until the horse actually leaves the ground. Note the sympathetic contact of the reins and the effort placed on the horse's tendons at the point of takeoff.   BRANT GAMMA

TOP RIGHT:

THE horse's arc has started to develop and Karen is following correctly with her upper body. Her lower leg has slipped back slightly as a result of her move up the horse's neck. She has closed her elbows to maintain contact with the reins, while still going forward with the body. BRANT GAMMA

BOTTOM RIGHT:

HERE Karen is beginning to replace her lower leg and to put the horse more in front of her in preparation for the landing. The elbows start to open as the horse stretches his head and neck out for the landing phase. BRANT GAMMA

*K*AREN is exactly where we would like to see her at this phase of the jump—lower leg in a slightly defensive place, hips low, weight centered behind her horse's shoulder, and reins supporting the horse's mouth in a straight line. BRANT GAMMA

*A*GAIN, you couldn't ask for anything better. Karen's knee is accepting the shock of the landing; her hips are behind the horse's shoulders; her shoulders are up; her eyes are looking for the next fence; and her elbows are opening, following the horse's head and mouth on into the landing phase. From the look on the horse's face, he obviously appreciates the ride that he's getting. While the length of rein has remained the same, Karen has opened and closed her elbows to maintain a following contact throughout the arc. Karen Lende on Innishkerry, North Georgia, 1992. BRANT GAMMA

*T*HIS fence had caused a lot of trouble throughout the day, and my instructions to Juliet were to "sit tight, make sure that you drive your horse across both hedges, and don't allow him to 'peep' at the ditch in between." Juliet is doing a great job of keeping the horse in front of her leg and at the end of her reins. She has put her lower leg in a defensive place without sitting completely. From the look on the horse's face he understands the situation and is going to land running. Juliet Graham on Jones, Ledyard, South Hamilton, Massachusetts, 1977. ALIX COLEMAN

down, while your body is poised and still from the waist up. Do not stiffen your knee or straighten your leg and take up the shock of the horse's gallop stride by waving your upper body at the horse. This causes you to work out of rhythm with the horse's stride and to unbalance the horse by continually moving from slightly in front of the motion to slightly behind the motion. Stay poised over the horse's center of gravity with the horse just in front of you, and take up the shock in the knee angle rather than in the waist.

At some point before the jump you should sit in a light three-point. Usually this is about eight strides away, but when my students are approaching a downhill jump, I advise them to sit a bit sooner, with slightly longer reins, and to be in a slightly more upright position. Sit a bit later, with shorter than normal reins, when approaching an uphill jump, so that your body does not exert a dragging effect on the horse's stride. The reason for sitting down in the approach to the jump is that it is very difficult to use your legs and your reins in an independent fashion when you are supporting yourself on your knees. Once you enter the saddle it becomes easy to use your reins, your legs, or, indeed, your whip, as the situation demands. Remember to enter the saddle softly and in rhythm with the horse's stride. Try not to bang down on the horse's kidneys, or fall back in the reins, as you reenter the saddle.

Review the experiment that I gave you on page 53 in the dressage section where you drop your stirrups, drop your reins, take your legs away from the sides of the horse, and then attempt to drive with your seat bones. This will remind you that your ability to have an effect on the horse with your seat bones is extremely limited. If you need impulsion in front of a fence, use your heels. If the heels are not enough, use your spurs. If the spurs are not enough, use your whip and your voice; but do not attempt to shove the horse into the jump by waving your upper body at him.

All this is going to do is cause the horse to become unbalanced and, therefore, less willing to go forward. Remember, keep the upper body still. Make the horse go forward with the lower leg, and come back with the reins.

Also remember that your ability to help the horse with the reins when galloping at speed is very limited. The horse has to balance himself. Probably one of the hardest lessons that the cross-country rider has to learn is to be, basically, out of control. You are

*A*FTER I saw Bill Steinkraus win an Olympic gold medal on a horse that "opened up" early over spread fences, I never worried about it again. Like Snowbound, this horse knows what he is doing. Early in the course the designer will give you some fences to get you galloping and allow you to settle your horse into a rhythm. Here David is doing exactly that. Placed in the center of his horse, with his legs on and ready to land galloping, David is in as good a position as you'll find. David O'Connor on Wilton Fair, World Championships, Stockholm, 1990. KARL LECK

HORSES make a terrific effort jumping up a bank. The rider has to make the same sort of effort to stay with the horse. The slightest backward inclination from Karen and this horse will catch her hind legs as she lands up the bank. Karen's lower leg could be a little further back. The upper body and reins are as good as they can get. Karen Lende on Mrs. Jacquiline Mars Vogel's Shannon, Punchestown, Ireland, 1993.

going to point the horse at jumps, you are going to dictate the overall speed, and, hopefully, you are going to be quite accurate about the line that you take both between jumps and in the approach to the next jump. Your ability to dictate to the horse where he puts his feet or exactly where he carries his head and neck is going to be quite limited. The proof of this lies in the success of very small female riders. If strength were the most important aspect of riding, then all of us would look like weight lifters, rather than the slim, trim outline that most good riders provide.

The reins should always have a knot at the end of them when going across country. This knot should be all the way back at the buckle, rather than forward against the rubber grips.

The reins are knotted for two reasons. First of all, the leather at the buckle is the narrowest part of the reins and thus the weakest . . . it already has a hole in it.

Second, by putting a knot in the reins, you will always know where the center of the reins is if you lose your reins, and you will know which way to go to straighten the neck as you pick up the reins. Practice slipping and regaining your reins while you are hacking. This will be good for your dressage anyway, as it will teach the horse to lengthen and shorten his stride at the walk without jigging when you try to pick up the reins.

Let the reins slip through your fingers as the horse's head and neck call for them. Do not just open your fingers and throw the reins away, but follow with the reins until the horse's head and neck have stopped moving forward.

You should follow the horse's mouth with the reins until your arms reach their full extension. If the horse is still reaching with his head and neck, you must follow by slipping the reins rather than by closing your waist angle. The minute you start to lean forward to follow the horse's mouth, you are putting yourself in a position to fall off.

Then, put the knot in your whip hand. Place your opposite hand just in front of your whip hand on top of both reins. Lift the whip hand back to the point of your shoulder and the other hand forward toward the points of the horse's ears. Do not push your hands down while picking up your reins as this will cause you to get tied up in the horse's mane, and you will fail to shorten the reins enough. It is better to overshorten and then slip the reins slightly to adjust them than it is not to shorten them enough. After your forward hand has reached its full extension, put that hand down on the neck, drop the knot with your whip hand, and regain your normal hold of the reins. (See photo caption on page 37.)

Cross-country riders should know how to use both a single and a double bridge. This is sometimes referred to as a single or a double "cross" of the reins. For example, take the whip in your right hand, then reach across and also hold the left rein in the right hand without letting go of the left rein with your left hand. This is referred to as a single cross. A double cross means that you have both reins in both hands. This is a stronger bridge but it is less easy to adjust and, therefore, I rarely use it across country. It can be used on horses that take a fierce hold during their training gallops. The single bridge can also be used as a safety device when jumping down big drops, or into deep water or muddy footing, where the rider can reasonably expect the horse to peck. Landing against the bridge can provide you with an extremely powerful balancing tool for your upper body. This trick has saved many a rider who otherwise would have gone off down the banister.

TRAINING THE HORSE

*C*ROSS-COUNTRY jumping is the hardest of the three disciplines to learn because the effect of the terrain and the speed make jumping so complex. At the same time, you can practice it the least because it is the most physically strenuous for the horse. The more you do of it, the less often you will be able to compete. As a result, I rarely school horses after the competition season has started unless the horse shows that he does not yet understand a particular problem that cross-country courses present, i.e., water, ditches, or coffins. If that is the case, I will take the horse back to an area that provides that particular problem and work with him until I am sure that he understands the nature of the questions that are being asked and the way to answer those questions.

There are three different ways of schooling a horse cross-country:

*C*ONSIDERING that I had only been out of a plaster leg cast for two weeks, this isn't a bad photo.

You should land from a drop as if you had jumped down yourself and wanted to land on your feet. My elbows have followed as far as they can, so I have to let the reins slip. Don't lean forward to follow your horse's mouth. The author on Kilkenny, Badminton, 1968. JEAN BRIDEL DE L'ANNÉE HIPPIQUE

I HAD so much confidence in Bill (The Optimist) that I am letting him sort out the result of overjumping into water while I look off at an angle for the next fence. Because my heel has slipped back, there is a slight forward rotation of my upper body. Fortunately, I save myself in the next stride by placing my bridge against my horse's neck and, indeed, go on to win my final three-day event. The author on Mr. and Mrs. Bertram Firestone's The Optimist, Rolex Kentucky, 1986.   PHELPS PHOTOGRAPHY

1. One way is to school a course. Find a local course where you can put together some sort of course at or below the level of your horse, hopefully about 1,600 meters with fifteen to twenty fences. Strike off at the speed of your level, and away you go. The advantage of this is that it provides the most realistic form of practice before a competition. It develops the most rhythm for the horse and rider, because once they get going they settle down and concentrate on jumping the next fence.

It is also the most strenuous on your horse's legs, however, and you should therefore do it the least. In addition, this type of schooling has the most deleterious effect on the horse's dressage and show jumping. The sharper the horse gets across country, the more difficult he is going to be to deal with in the dressage arena. While this is one of the fascinating problems of training three-event horses, it is certainly one you should avoid if possible.

2. I refer to the second sort of cross-country schooling as "fence by fence." This means exactly what it says. You wander out to a cross-country area, and, after warming the horse up for fifteen to twenty minutes, you find some easy fences to jump over, then some more difficult fences, then some combinations, then some easier fences, then, possibly, the sort of fence that your horse finds the most difficult—whether ditches, water, or whatever—then a few big galloping fences and then a few easy fences to finish up.

Again, the horse should jump between fifteen and twenty obstacles. He can repeat a few of them if you are not satisfied with his performance over them. But, basically, go to the jump at the speed of your level and take what you get. The advantage of this type of schooling is that it is easier on the legs of the horse because you are covering less distance at the gallop. It is certainly easier on the coach as he can see you jump every cross-country fence, which is not the case when you are doing a course or, indeed, at a competition.

The disadvantages are that you may have trouble developing your rhythm when you school in a stop-and-go fashion. However, this may be a good thing if you have a horse that is

*N*O one knows more about riding across country than Lucinda. Look at the lovely contact with her horse's mouth. The placement of her lower leg allows her to be delicate in the use of her reins. Because her stirrups are adjusted correctly, she can sit back without sitting down. The expression on this horse's face says it all. Lucinda Green on Brass Monkey.   BRIAN HILL

*I*N this photograph I'm on a young horse that had a tendency to jump up in the air, rather than across. Therefore, I have closed my heels and softened the reins, trying to encourage her to jump across the fence more. While I have lowered my hips, I have not sat down on the horse's back, which could destroy the arc that I'm trying to create here. The author on Mr. and Mrs. Paul A. Seymour's Lawrecean, Debroke Trophy, Blue Ridge, Boyce, Virginia, 1975.   GAMECOCK PHOTO

*P*ADDY has gotten a little bit close to the bank, so I have increased the rein contact off the ground, and kept my leg under my body. Although I have lifted my hips off the horse's back, I have not gone very far forward up his neck as I want to wait and see whether he rubs the fence or not before I follow. The author on Mr. and Mrs. Richard Thompson's Castlewellan, Olympic Selection Trials, Rolex Kentucky, 1984. PHELPS PHOTOGRAPHY

very hot and tense. Schooling in what I call "stop-and-go traffic" may be just the thing to keep your horse from boiling over. As an aside, schooling over an entire course may be just the sort of thing to do if your horse is sluggish in dressage. Sometimes this will make your horse pick up the bridle and want to go forward. Whatever the type of horse, make sure that you go well away from the fences before striking off, so that you have settled into a rhythm before you approach the fence with the horse. Second, make sure that you school at the speed of your level. Make yourself school at 520 meters per minute if you are going to go to a Preliminary event. Make yourself school at 570 meters per minute if that is the speed of your level. This does not hold true for combinations and fences that need to be show-jumped. But whenever you have a fence that can be jumped at the speed of your level, make sure to jump it at that speed.

3. The third way to school a horse cross-country is to use gymnastic cross-country fences. One of the difficulties of schooling cross-country is that the rider or trainer cannot adjust the height and spread of the cross-country fence. This leads to a certain "do or die" attitude on the part of the rider that I think, in these modern times, is a bit unnecessary.

Many of the problems that you are going to confront during a cross-country course can be simulated at home using portable standards and rustic rails. Just as in show jumping exercises, if you start with a very low fence and explain to the horse what it is that he is going to do, many times you'll find that horses can handle exercises of a very technical nature. However, you must remember to keep the exercises low at first, and set the distances so the horse can handle the fence from the trot. Then, as the height of the fence increases, and more important, as the horse remains calm, change the distances and approach at the canter.

One advantage of cross-country gymnastics is that it allows you to jump more often because you are mostly jumping at the trot over lower fences. It also gives you a chance to analyze and practice over simulations of specific problems, such as ditches, banks, or water. New and unusual combination of corners,

*T*HIS position is a little bit casual. I wonder what would happen if the horse stumbled or missed his landing. But when you have a horse as good as Paddy, you tend to find yourself in this kind of shape. Things rarely went wrong on the cross-country course with him. I'd like the lower leg slightly more forward and the body more erect for safety. The author on Mr. and Mrs. Richard Thompson's Castlewellan, Olympic Selection Trials, Ships Quarters, Westminster, Maryland, 1984. PHELPS PHOTOGRAPHY

*D*ON'T let your lower leg slip back when you're jumping a big drop. The only thing that saved me here was the backward inclination of my upper body and my knee grip. There would be nothing in front of me if Henry (Kilkenny) had slipped or stumbled. The author on Kilkenny, World Championships, Punchestown, Ireland, 1970. PETER SWEETMAN

*J*UMPING narrow fences is very much the wave of the future. In course design a narrow fence requires a precise, balanced approach and very skillful, technical riding in order to negotiate it successfully. Here Jill is displaying the superb lower leg position and balance that brought her to the top so quickly. It is interesting to note how often riders with a strong lower leg position have soft, sensitive hands. Compare this photo with the photo on page 105 and see the sensitive hold of the hands on the reins. Jill Walton on Patrona, Olympics, Barcelona, 1992. KARL LECK

*T*HIS is pretty much the shape I want you to land in over big drops. The stability of my position is based on landing with my feet underneath me. Rather than worrying about falling off, I can devote all of my energies to getting the horse out over the next, rather narrow fence. Stirrups one hole shorter would have kept my seat completely out of the saddle. You can tell from the focus of my head and eyes where I'm going next. The author on Mr. and Mrs. Bertram Firestone's The Optimist, Lexington, 1986. PHELPS PHOTOGRAPHY

ditches, water, bounces, corner bounces—anything that the course designer's fertile mind can produce—can be duplicated by you with portable rails and standards.

As an example of how to use these schooling exercises, assume that you have a small ditch on level ground. Place a pair of standards on either side of the ditch with no rails on the ground yet. Trot and canter back and forth over the ditch until the horse will jump it fairly calmly on a long or, if possible, a loose rein.

Now put your first rail on the ground, and approach in the direction of home or the out gate, so that the horse jumps the rail and steps over the ditch going in his favorite direction. If you are jumping at the trot, you can put a 9-foot placing rail before the jump and start to raise it. Basically, you should come once from the right and once from the left over each height at which you set the rail. After the rail has reached 2 feet 6 inches to 3 feet you can add a rail on the other side of the ditch at the same height with a placing rail 9 feet on the other side of that. You now have an exercise that the horse can trot through both ways.

The distance from the edge of the ditch to the rails will vary with the size of the ditch and the speed that you are riding. Eighteen feet should probably be sufficient on each side while you are trotting over this exercise. Later on if you wish to school at the canter with the rail higher, you will need to make the distance from 21 to 24 feet. Try to jump this exercise on as loose a rein as possible. If the horse is very difficult to control, you are probably better off working at the trot rather than going on to the canter and increasing your grip on the reins. Get the horse to relax, think for himself, and use his own initiative. He must feel free to save you from any situation that he may get you into.

This is an excellent schooling exercise for coffins as, at some point during the session, the horse is going to lose his concentration over the first rail and start thinking about the ditch and the second rail. While this causes some form of a disaster on a cross-country course, it causes only a knockdown in this situation and the horse should be quite willing to come around, rectify his mistake, and jump both fences well the next time. The horse will learn from knocking down a rail. It is hard for him to learn anything good from a wreck.

*W*HEN you are the "lead-off batter" for a team, your only thought is "Don't fall off." Here Don has obviously decided that, if he makes a mistake, it will be too far back, not too far forward.

If your reins get too tight when landing over a drop, your horse will pull you off over his shoulders as his head and neck go forward. Once again, a correct leg position allows soft reins.

It kind of spoils a coach when his first working-student spends two years with him and goes off and wins a gold medal. Don Sachey on the USET's Plain Sailing, World Championships, Burghley, Stamford, Lincs, England, 1974. WERNER ERNST

*W*HILE it's nice to be young and brave, I suspect that the speed of the approach has been a bit rapid. However, the security of Derek's lower leg position and the natural athletic ability of his horse are going to see him through the water in fine style. The reins should be slipped just a bit more, and the upper body more upright. Derek diGrazia on Thriller II, Rolex Kentucky, 1982. GAMECOCK PHOTO

*W*HEN jumping a large drop late in the course the three-day event rider must be defensive. Basically, my attitude here is that it's going to take a bomb to dislodge me from the middle of my horse. The placement of my foot in front of my knee gives me some extra leverage, and my seat is just out of the saddle. Don't sit on your horse's back at this point, or you will cause him to rub his stifles and hocks as he drops over the rail. As it is, I barely have enough margin for Pop to clear this rail behind. The author on Carawich, World Championships, Lexington, 1978. BARRY KAPLAN

The same procedure can be used to school banks and water. Set up the basic aspect of the exercise first. That is to say, trot the horse on a long rein back and forth across a bank that you are going to use. When the horse becomes accustomed to the bank and relaxed about jumping it, start placing rails on the ground. Because of the variations in terrain, footing, and size of our cross-country jumps, it is difficult to give exact distances for these gymnastics. You are much better off to begin by putting a rail on the ground and trotting back and forth over it. Feel whether the horse is going to be comfortable at that distance, or whether you should move it in or bring it out. After you become adept at using these exercises, you can start to produce very long distances and very short distances. Your first emphasis should be on producing a horse that jumps calmly, fluidly, and in a forward fashion, always seeking the next obstacle on a slightly opening stride.

While using gymnastic cross-country jumping, you will run into the same problems that you encounter while training horses for show jumping. Cross-country horses are going to stop, rush, drift— all of the problems that we see in show jumping. Deal with them in the same manner. If your horse is rushing through a rail-bank-rail exercise, put rails on the ground in between the rail and the bank and, again, between the bank and the rail. This will cause many horses to slow down and assess their landing point much more carefully.

If the horse continues to rush, put a double bounce at one end of the exercise and trot toward it from the opposite end. It's very easy for a horse to rush through a single bounce. It is quite difficult for him to rush through a double or even a triple bounce. If he rushes into the first part of the bounce, he will leave his shoulders behind and be in the wrong shape to jump out. If you are going to resort to this, make sure to lower the rails first so that the horse at least survives the experience.

The design and complexity of gymnastic exercises are limitless. Once you have introduced a concept to your horse there is no end to the things that you can teach him. The challenge is not to get too carried away with these exercises, as it can make the horse a bit befuddled. I also wonder if too much overly technical schooling might not make your horse a bit unwilling to jump his fences from a forward rhythm.

Apply these three ways of schooling cross-country courses differently to different horses. Very hot horses will, obviously, benefit tremendously from using gymnastic jumping and schooling fence by fence, rather than being allowed to go ripping around a cross-country course. Very dopey, half-blood horses probably should do a bit of gymnastic jumping but, for the most part, they should be allowed to gallop over at least six or eight fences at a time in order to get their blood up and make them take an interest in what they are doing. Here, as everywhere else, the intuition and common sense of the rider has to take precedence over prior assumptions about the training of the cross-country horse.

STEEPLECHASE

*I*F you are going to your first three-day event, you must find an area where you can practice the steeplechase phase. This should be plugged in to your schedule and should be viewed as a gallop day. You are going to stress the horse's lungs as well as his legs during this period, and you have to plan for this just as you would any other intensive conditioning work. Make sure that the footing is as good as possible where you are going to school. If you have to, see whether you can construct a couple of rudimentary brush fences on a local Thoroughbred conditioning track and school there, rather than galloping over rough or hard turf. The little bit of extra work will be worth it. One of the greatest compliments you will ever receive is when your horse trots out for the first vet inspection and an appreciative murmur comes out of the crowd at the obvious well-being of your horse.

After fifteen or twenty minutes of trot, the horse should be given at least a four-minute canter at 400 meters a minute to warm up. Then, assuming that you have a half-mile track, I would gallop around over the fences for about a mile at anywhere from 450 to 520 meters a minute. Concentrate on showing the horse the jumps, letting him feel the brush and realize that the box is quite low and that he can safely jump through the top of the fence. After the horse has warmed up over the jumps three or four times, you should then ride for a mile at the speed of your competitive level. This means that, in addition to going to the trouble of stuffing the portable jumps with brush and bringing them to the conditioning track or the galloping area, you need to have measured off with a meter wheel a known distance and computed the time in which you should gallop that distance, so that you will know what the speed of your steeplechase phase feels like to you while you are competing.

Do not attempt to produce fantastic, long strides. Do not check the horse frantically to the bottom of the fence. Attempt to jump the fence from the same rhythm that you approached it and to land at the same speed that you jumped it. Try not to lose time over the fence in the air but to maintain a steady, regular speed throughout.

I DON'T like to think of the steeplechase phase as the place to throw in enormous, energy-wasting leaps. But when you have a horse with an attitude like Kilkenny's, all you can do is sit still and keep things together. Nobody was going to tell Kilkenny how to do a steeplechase course; and, if you tried to, you would lose more energy wrestling with him than you would save by slowing him down. The author on Kilkenny, Olympics, Mexico City, 1968. WERNER ERNST

Especially at the gallop the rider's ability to lengthen and shorten the frame of the horse is extremely limited. At that point the bit is not a means of controlling the stride, but rather is a balancing aid for the horse. Those of you who have ever seen a circus high-wire artist carry a bamboo pole are watching the same process. When we pull against the bit we are really using something that we

*T*HIS is a great position for timber racing or steeplechasing unless something goes wrong. You need much more angle at your knee and a more defensive position of your upper body to survive any sort of mistake when traveling at a high rate of speed over fixed fences. The author on Mrs. John W. Wofford's Malakasia, New Jersey Hunt Cup, Far Hills, 1969. FREUDY PHOTOS

are part of. Instead of thinking that we can pull and brace against the bamboo pole, we must use it to produce minor shifts in our center of gravity so that we can continue along a straight and narrow path in balance. Major alterations in the placement of the bamboo pole are going to cause us to lose our balance further rather than to regain it.

FURTHER SCHOOLING

*O*NCE the horse and rider have successfully completed their first three-day event, I rarely go back and school the horse again over steeplechase fences. Our horses are good jumpers. They're not going to be taken aback by a set of four brush jumps twice around, and the more you gallop fast on a horse, the more difficult he is going to be to ride on the flat or over show jumps, and the shorter his soundness period is going to be. I never do anything strenuous with the horse that I don't have to do in order to prepare him for a three-day event.

As a final note, when riding in a three-day event think of the steeplechase phase in a negative fashion, rather than a positive one. In a steeplechase race the obvious point is to go as fast as you can for as long as you can and beat everyone else. In phase B of the three-day event the attitude of the rider should be that you want to go as slowly as possible and still make the time. Remember that every ounce of energy that you take out of the horse on the steeplechase phase will not be available to you at the end of the cross-country phase. Save your horse as much as possible. Hug the turns. Ask for fences where the horse jumps out of rhythm, rather than driving down to the jump and producing awe-inspiring, long, flat strides, which leave both the crowd, and the horse, gasping for breath.

Avoid getting your horse too flat on the steeplechase. In half an hour to forty-five minutes, he is going to come back and jump obstacles made out of solid materials. You want your horse to be jumping with a good shape when it approaches obstacles of that type. The steeplechase phase is not the time to start to teach your horse how to be a racehorse. Phase B should be viewed as a place to protect your horse's energies rather than expend them.

*T*HE late John Harty, a member of the Irish three-day event team for the 1964 Tokyo Olympics, was born with an instinctive feel for the middle of his horse. When your coach tells you to let the horse jump out in front of you, this is what he's talking about. The impeccable lower leg position allows John (Number 17 in this picture) to remain balanced and maintain a sensitive feel of the reins, on a horse that is jumping in an incredible fashion. John Harty on Fort Ord, Naas, Ireland, 1975.   LIAM HEALY

*W*HEN you send your horse forward to a fence, don't drop the reins. Because Ann has kept hold of her reins, the horse's head and neck are elevating while the hindquarters are engaging. Ann's leg is slightly behind her because she is determined to keep her leg on until her horse leaves the ground. Compare this photo with the one on page 127. Both show the same rein contact and leg position, but I like Ann's more erect upper body better. You get mixed emotions when your students start to show you up. Ann Hardaway-Taylor on Commissar, Badminton, 1992. BRANT GAMMA

*W*HEN it is late in the course you must override. Even though we are landing on level ground, I have a firm grip on the reins, a single bridge, and my leg in a very defensive place. You can tell from the strain in my arms and my face that I'm beginning to work to keep things together. Horses don't ride the same at the end of twenty miles of speed and endurance as they do at the end of a two-mile horse trials course. You must learn to compensate for your horse's fatigue by riding more aggressively and defensively. The author on Carawich, Alternate Olympics, Fontainebleau, France, 1980.   FINDLAY DAVIDSON

*T*HIS is how you make the optimum time over a giant course—one stride away from the fence, and still galloping. Horses usually back off water, so your attitude has to be aggressive. It is much easier to survive a mistake caused by aggression than to get out of a situation caused by timidity. Although Karen's foot is home in the stirrup, her weight is still down in the ankle. This security allows her to be confident and supple in her upper body and reins. Karen Lende on Mr. Richard Thompson's Mr. Maxwell, Badminton, 1992. BRANT GAMMA

*I*F you could tell a cross-country rider only one thing, it would be "stay behind the motion." Here Jill may have gone back slightly early but there's no doubt in your mind that, when she lands in the middle of a very difficult water complex, she's going to be in total control of the situation. Jill Walton on Patrona, Olympics, Barcelona, 1992.

*T*HIS series was taken at the Water Complex at the World Championships, Lexington, 1978. In the first frame you can see that I am making sure to keep my leg on, keep a rein support, and yet stay behind the horse's shoulders with my upper body. Never underestimate the fact that your horse is going to react to big fences. If you get used to being towed around small courses, you will be taken aback when your horse suddenly begins to react to the size of the jump. If you are going to make a mistake, override, don't underride. BRANT GAMMA

I'M right where I want to be at this stage of the proceedings. My leg is on at the girth; my reins have not started to slip yet; and I'm looking forward, waiting to see how Carawich is going to react once he jumps onto the bank. BRANT GAMMA

I'M in trouble now as his hind leg has slipped back down the bank. I have kept my legs on at the girth, lowered my hips saddle, and ridden him forward into a steady hand, while Pop solves the problem for me. BRANT GAMMA

AFTER taking a shuffle stride, Pop is leaving the ground. I am driving my heel in to make sure that he doesn't suspect for an instant that I don't want to jump in there. While I have drawn my hands closer to my body in order to maintain contact with his mouth as he leaves the ground, there isn't any inclination of my upper body forward. When in doubt, wait it out. BRANT GAMMA

I CAN feel that Pop is going, so I slip the reins without committing my upper body. The water is quite deep and I'm expecting a tremendous shock when I land. I want to make sure that I start down into the water in a defensive position, with my leg moving in front of me.
BRANT GAMMA

I'VE done everything that I can to get the horse into the water well. Because I'm worried about it I'm sitting too much, and this is going to catch up with me in a couple of frames. At this point my seat should still be above the saddle. I think that sitting in the air, as I have done here, causes the horse to catch his ankles on the log just before he lands, which will start my shoulders forward too soon.   BRANT GAMMA

*W*ELCOME to the major leagues. Rubbing the log behind has started to snap my upper body forward and my heels back. Now I'm a fugitive from the law of averages. The only thing that can save me, at this point, is the strength of my bridge, and the power and balance of my horse. BRANT GAMMA

*T*HANK heavens for a strong knot at the end of my reins, as I am able to push myself back off the horse's neck and continue across the complex. It helps that Pop explodes up out of the water. If I had landed with my feet in front of me and my seat out of the saddle, I would not be in this predicament. BRANT GAMMA

*D*ON'T waste time thinking about how lucky you were, think about what to do next. Having survived a fairly interesting moment, I'm putting Pop back on his line and helping him to get out of a formidable complex. The author on Carawich, World Championships, Lexington, 1978. BRANT GAMMA

ONE of America's best all-around horsemen, Kevin is showing here the balance and sensitivity that took him to three Olympics and three silver medals. Not many people can ride as wide a range of horses as Kevin has, either in eventing, racing over timber, or show jumping. Here he is pushing a slightly tired Good Mixture over the last fence in the Olympics. The closing of his lower leg has caused a slight displacement of his position, but the overall impression is so genuine that it is hard to complain. Kevin Freeman on Good Mixture, Olympics, Munich, 1972. GAMECOCK PHOTO

6

Show Jumping

THE usual show jumping test takes place on level ground and at a greatly reduced speed from that of cross-country. Since the first rule of any type of jumping is not to fall off, the security of the rider's seat is of paramount importance. In order to understand the position you will use on the horse, we should first study the way the horse jumps.

The jumping form of the horse is often referred to as the "bascule." Bascule is a French word which refers to the arc that the horse describes with his body in the air over a fence. Therefore, we can have good bascules; we can have bad bascules; hopefully, we won't have no bascule. Although we notice a horse's flawed jumping technique in the air, the flaw usually can be traced back to the approach or the takeoff. For example, often horses that are flat in the air are too fast in the approach.

If every horse describes a bascule with his body in the air, what should we look for when we look for a horse with a good bascule?

The horse takes off for a fence from a distance that equals the height of the fence. He describes a perfect half circle from that point, reaching the top part of his arc over the highest point of the fence and landing at a distance from the fence that also equals its height. We would like to see the forearms drawn above the horizontal, both knees level, and the shoulders brought up and forward in a soft, easy, fluid motion. The head and neck should drop and round at the top of the arc. The hindquarters should be level; the hocks should engage in the air under the body and then return to the ground with a smooth, flowing motion in sequence behind the landing of the forelegs.

The most important part of the bascule is the point of takeoff. This is the point at which the horse's forward momentum is transformed into a jumping effort. Note that at the point of takeoff the motion of the horse is going straight up. This knowledge gives you a couple of very powerful analytical tools. Although an oversimplification, it is true that the horse produces the height of the jump with his shoulders and the arc of the jump with his hindquarters.

Thus, when things are not going well in the show jumping phase, you can start to analyze why. If your horse is knocking rails down in front, he probably is rushing on the forehand. Slow the approach. If the horse is knocking fences down behind, or is jumping with a smooth, flowing arc up to the peak and then falling out of the sky like a dead duck, he is probably not pushing off with his hindquarters. Use more leg off the ground.

Any jumping effort, whether it is steeplechase, show jumping, or cross-country, contains five separate and distinct phases. These are: (1) the approach, (2) the takeoff, (3) the flight, (4) the landing, and (5) the departure. Regardless of the type of jumping discipline, the jump effort of the horse will show these five phases:

1. *The approach.* The approach should be made in a light, three-point seat with your shoulders just in advance of your hips, an arch in the small of your back, your weight in the ankles, and a straight line from your elbow to the horse's mouth. Occasionally you will find horses that perform better when the approach is made in a two-point, but these are the exception rather than the rule.

Most horses will go better with a slight support from the rider's seat and leg. Your position should not change from the initial approach to the final approach. Every time you change your position you change the horse's balance. The key to jumping well is to arrive at the fence in a good takeoff spot with a horse that is in balance. Therefore, take care not to disturb the horse's balance as he approaches the fence. Make your alterations in speed, balance, and length of stride as far back from the fence as possible.

2. *The takeoff.* Resist the temptation to throw yourself ahead of the motion here. The first part of the jumping effort actually goes straight up, not forward. Your seat bones must remain on the saddle until the horse's forefeet leave the ground. At this point the benefit of a slightly forward position of the upper body becomes apparent. The strength of the horse's jump will push you up into the correct place in the air, rather than your having to force yourself there.

3. *The flight.* The horse's back must be allowed unlimited freedom from the time that his forefeet leave the ground in front of the fence until the time that they touch the ground on the opposite side of the fence. You must stay in a two-point throughout the flight phase of the jumping effort. Your ability to influence the horse is limited while the horse is in the air. Any signal that we give the horse in terms of slowing down or speeding up has to wait for a response until the horse's feet touch the ground. Most especially, a frantic tugging on the reins in the air is only going to cause the horse to land even more on his forehand. Be part of the solution, don't be part of the problem.

4. *The landing.* It is here that the shock-absorbing function of the knee becomes apparent. Riders who topple over or fall back too soon are going to cause the horse to land out of balance. The best place to land is with your weight going down directly into your knee joint, continuing on through a vertical stirrup leather into the ankles. Any exaggerated deviation from this position should be avoided.

5. *The departure.* Your position in the departure from a fence should be identical to the position that was used in the approach. The horse should maintain its balance and rhythm, not speeding up or slowing down. You should land with the same length of rein and proceed away from the jump at the same pace and in the same frame as in the approach.

As in all training of the horse, when you run into show jumping difficulties, stop and analyze what is going wrong. Then make a plan, reset the jumping exercise, and try a slightly different technique based on the feel that you have just received from the horse during the last exercise. Probably the most frustrating type of student for a coach to work with is one who will continue to repeat his mistakes. Make all the mistakes you want, but make new mistakes. Don't practice bad habits.

THE SHOW JUMPING POSITION

*T*HE foundation of the rider's jumping position is in the stirrups. The stirrups substitute for the ground while we are suspended over the horse's back. They must always be kept in a position that guarantees our safety and stability.

The ball of the foot should be on the tread of the stirrup with enough pressure on the big toe to allow the sole of the boot to turn out slightly. The heel should be depressed so that the ankle is lower than the toes at all times. The foot and lower leg should describe a slight angle away from the horse's spine, and the stirrup leather should be maintained in a vertical position at all times. Do not turn your foot parallel to the horse and press against your little toe, as it will cause your lower leg to slip back. While the heel should never be at the same level as the toes, it should not be jammed down so far as to cause the joint to lock. The ankle should stay in the middle of its range of motion.

Distribute your leg grip equally from the inside point of the knee to the inside point of the ankle. The grip should only concentrate in one area when an effect is desired. For example, horses that are slow off the ground need much firmer heel pressure and possibly support from the spur and/or stick. This encourages them to follow through with their hindquarters and produce a bascule that is balanced in front and behind the jump.

If your horse has produced an awkward effort, or you are becoming dislodged for one reason or another, concentrate on maintaining your knee grip. It is amusing but true that if you do not lose your knee grip, you will never fall off. You may get in some strange and awkward shapes on the horse's back; but as long as the horse maintains his feet, you will stay in the saddle. If 90 percent of success in life is just showing up, 90 percent of success in riding is not falling off.

The knee is the strongest joint in the rider's body. Coaches speak a great deal of accepting the shock of landing in the ankles. This is correct as far as it goes, but it does not describe completely what happens as the horse and rider return to the ground. The ability of a joint to accept shock is limited by the size and strength of the joint. The majority of the shock of landing must be accepted in the knee joint. Therefore, it is essential that the rider jump with stirrups adjusted so as to create a spring. Before jumping, occasionally have a friend or bystander examine your stirrup lengths to make sure you have the correct length of stirrup. When the rider is seated in the saddle with jumping length stirrups, there should be at least a 90-degree angle between the thigh and the lower leg. Too long a stirrup will lead to severe idiosyncrasies in your upper body position. Too short a stirrup can lead to toppling over or getting left, depending on the jumping effort of the horse. A correctly adjusted stirrup puts you in the middle of the horse's jumping motion. To find the correct stirrup length for show jumps up to 3 feet 6 inches, drop your stirrups at the halt. Let both legs hang straight down, with no angle at the knee. The tread of the stirrup should strike you at, or just above, your ankle bone. Check your stirrup length at least once a month because your stirrup leather may stretch.

The hip joint should be sufficiently closed to maintain your shoulders slightly in advance of your hip. In addition there should be a slight forward arch in the small of the back at all times. The purpose for this is that, when the shoulders are slightly in front of the hips and the back is arched, you are in the best shape to receive the jumping effort.

From this configuration the jumping effort will push your upper body forward into the correct two-point position in the air without appreciable effort on your part. This is especially true over fences lower than 3 feet 6 inches. Past that you need to supply some effort. But for the majority of fences that you will jump in your career, a quiet, waiting, balanced approach will place you in balance with the horse in the air. Your head and neck should be up and

SOME horses haven't read the book, and you have to explain to them that it is terrifically important to you that they jump clean today. I have just finished giving Bill a half-halt and am now pushing his head and neck forward and around the back rail of the oxer with my reins, while trying to keep some leg on him in the air. From the expression on my horse's face he understands what I am trying to convey but is not terribly impressed. By dint of much moving around in the saddle I was able to convince Bill to produce a clean round, but it wasn't pretty. The author on Mr. and Mrs. Bertram Firestone's The Optimist, Rolex Kentucky, 1986. ROBERT STRAUS

erect. Your upper body should never be used to initiate the jumping effort. Do not snap forward on landing, or topple back, but remain poised above the horse's back.

The following action of the body is something that you should be able to produce, especially over low fences, without using the reins. Occasional exercises, such as jumping without reins, jumping with arms outstretched down a gymnastic line, and so on, go a long way toward establishing a sound jumping foundation. Once this following action of your body is established, you may then add contact with the reins.

All of us have heard the comment "this rider has good hands" or "that rider has terrible hands over a jump." The ability of the hand to physically follow the horse's mouth is actually quite limited. What we are seeing when the rider correctly follows the horse's mouth is a relaxation of the shoulder, which allows the upper arm to pivot. Then a spring is maintained from the back of the rider's elbow through the reins to the horse's mouth. Done correctly, this contact never varies throughout the five phases of the jump. In reality, as I mentioned earlier, we should not refer to a rider as having "good hands" but rather "good elbows" or "good shoulders."

The adjustment of the reins should not vary. If you are landing with longer reins than when you took off, you are probably losing your lower leg position. If you topple back with your body, you should slip the reins to keep from punishing the horse's mouth. Check the length of your stirrup, reestablish a vertical line in the stirrup leather throughout the five phases, keep more weight in the ankles, and tighten your knee grip. You will find that you are able then to land above your knees, rather than slipping back and loosening the reins. Once the rein has been adjusted correctly the placement of the hand becomes critical.

Maintain a straight line from the back of the elbow to the horse's mouth. This assures the most direct and efficient contact. Beware of fads in the horse world such as hands elevated in a false attempt to elevate the horse's forehand, or hands which are placed below a straight line to the horse's mouth, which cause the rider to topple over and, occasionally, fall off. (I personally have nothing against fads. They cause incredible problems in the riders' performance and, sooner or later, they come to me for a lesson or clinic.)

Adopt a classical position, resist all fads and gadgets, and ride the horse quietly and softly between the two straight lines of the stirrup leather and the elbow to the horse's mouth. It's simple. It's just not easy.

POSITION FLAWS

*T*HERE are various flaws in the rider's jumping position which may appear from time to time. These flaws fall into categories and can usually be dealt with using the assistance of a competent observer. You should remember that the stirrup substitutes for the ground. Thus, the placement of the lower leg is critical throughout the jumping effort. For every action there is an equal and opposite reaction. For example, if the lower leg slips back, your upper body will topple over on landing. If your lower leg is stuck out in front of the girth, you will get left behind. Usually the flaws that we see in a rider's upper body position can be traced back to some error in the foundation of the rider's jumping seat. Don't look at the symptom, look for the cure. Improve the lower leg position.

1. *Toppling over.* If you land and have the feeling that you are about to go "down the banister," it is usually because the weight has come out of the ankles and the lower leg has slipped behind the vertical. Check to make sure that the stirrups are adjusted properly and work on keeping the foot at the girth. If you still topple over on landing, jump a few fences with your feet in front of the girth. This will usually cure the problem.

2. *Getting left.* On the other hand, if you consistently get left behind, you are probably going to the fence with your foot in front of your knee. This causes your shoulders to go backward when the horse leaves the ground. Bringing the lower leg back to the girth and maintaining the correct leg position in the approach will put you in a more balanced position at the point of takeoff. Occasionally the habit is so bad that the rider must work with the stirrups tied 6 inches from the girth.

3. *Collapsing in mid-air.* This is usually caused not by losing your lower leg position, but rather by taking the weight

I ASKED Shannon to show me what happens to a young horse in cavalletti when the rider gets in front of the motion. Here in the first frame she is in a nice shape but starting to lean forward and bring her heel back behind her. BRANT GAMMA

*B*ECAUSE I made Shannon lean too far forward, her horse begins to sprawl. As Smitty begins his takeoff motion the reins are a bit too soft and the inclination of the body is a little bit too far forward. This causes the reins to become quite loose upon landing and the heel to start sliding farther back. The rider is, basically, a passenger at this point. BRANT GAMMA

*I*N sending the horse forward to the second fence the leg is being displaced. Notice the heel is behind the hip; the seat bones are collapsing, and the reins are too soft. The overall appearance of the horse is downhill, even though the ring is level. BRANT GAMMA

*T*HE results of landing in front of the horse are apparent. The horse is falling toward the next jump, Shannon's reins are too soft, her body is too forward, and her leg is too far back. BRANT GAMMA

$\mathscr{A}$LTHOUGH the horse's forehand is still on the ground, Shannon has left the saddle. Notice the loop in the reins and the exaggerated forward posture of the body at the point of takeoff.   BRANT GAMMA

$\mathscr{T}$HE anticipation of the rider with her upper body has caused the horse to load his forehand and twist, giving a sprawled sensation to the jump. Shannon Brooks on General Lion, Fox Covert Farm, Upperville, Virginia, 1993.   BRANT GAMMA

out of the heels. When your subconscious knows that there is nothing solid to land on, you will collapse the knee joint in order to have the seat bones low to the saddle at the point of landing. Work on jumping small fences while remaining in a two-point. This will usually reestablish the security of your lower leg position.

4. *Ducking.* This slang term refers to a rider snapping his body to one side or the other of the horse's neck, thus losing his alignment over the horse's body. The rider's spine should remain centered over the horse's spine throughout the jumping effort. Ducking is caused when you place too much weight in the stirrup to the side where you duck and take the weight out of the opposite stirrup. This habit can usually be cured by removing the stirrup on the side that you duck toward. Following this, you will usually duck only one more time before finding a new source of security in what was a moment ago your weak leg! A few repetitions of jumping at the canter with only one stirrup over small fences will usually reestablish you in the center of the horse.

5. *Snapping back.* This habit is usually formed after you have toppled over for years. You now protect yourself by snapping your upper body violently backward at the point of landing. To correct this habit, work in a two-point holding on to a strap placed a third of the way up the horse's neck from the withers. Practice until you feel the security of landing correctly again, rather than whipping your body violently forward and back during the jumping motion.

6. *Jumping ahead.* This is usually caused initially by a length of stirrup which is slightly too long. If you do not have a 90-degree angle at the knee, there is insufficient spring to allow you to follow with the upper body. This habit can usually be cured by riding with a long riding whip in front of the elbows and behind the back. You will experience some difficulty with this exercise until you learn to follow the jumping motion with your knee and hip angles rather than with your upper body. The minute you follow with your upper body more erect and land over your knees and ankles, jumping will become easy once again.

Whatever the error in the rider's position, it can always be traced to a lack of support in the rider's lower leg. In riding, as in all else, the foundation of the edifice determines its strength. When you wish to analyze the rider's upper body position, look in the lower leg. That is where the problems in jumping positions truly begin.

One of my favorite exercises to show riders their correct position is to tie their stirrups to the girth with a 6-inch loop of string so that the stirrup hangs in a natural position. (Do not tie the stirrup *directly* against the girth.) Then place a neck strap over the horse, adjusted to where the rider's hands should be when he is in a correct two-point. Now allow the rider to canter around, jumping small jumps with the stirrups tied to the girth and the hands remaining in the neck strap as well as holding the reins. The rider will have trouble in the landing if he has snapped back. The stirrups are in the correct place; the hands are "handcuffed" in the correct place by the neck strap; it is now up to the rider to make his body conform to those two fixed points, by making his body come forward to his hands. The rider will find that, by having the stirrups at the girth at all times, the security of the upper body will immediately improve.

THE EYES OF THE HORSE

*B*EFORE we proceed to a description of various show jumping exercises, it is essential to understand the relationship between a horse's carriage and his vision. The horse sees using monocular vision. This means that his eye has a very limited range of motion in the socket. The horse adjusts his focus by raising and lowering his head and opening and closing the angle at the poll. The horse sees in the best focus along a line drawn 10 degrees in front of the plane of his nose. Considering that the horse was designed by nature to graze, it should not surprise us that the horse sees the ground very clearly. If you have turned a horse out in the paddock and watched it canter away, then stop, snort, raise its head and neck, and poke its nose in order to survey the horizon, you will have observed the process of a horse changing his focal point from near to far.

The reason I make this point is that it is essential that the horse see the jump. If we accept this as a major premise, then it follows that the rider must turn his efforts toward presenting the horse to the jump in balance rather than by attempting to bring the horse to the jump "on the bit."

An attempt to do the latter will actually restrict the ability of the horse to observe and evaluate the jump that it approaches. Most horses vigorously resist attempts to bring them to the jump with the plane of their face at the vertical. This is usually misunderstood by riders as resistance. Instead, it should be viewed as self-preservation.

In dressage lessons, I have often used the analogy that the body of the horse should be thought of as a giant spring. We maintain the tension on the spring in front with the reins and increase the energy by riding with our legs from behind. This is quite a useful analogy for dressage riders, but I think it is detrimental for show jumping, as it places too much emphasis on the reins and not enough on self-carriage.

The analogy that show jump riders should use is not that of a spring, but rather that of a "teeter-totter." Most of us have ridden a balance beam on a school playground. Think to yourself that, even if your horse is stiff as a board, you are not trying to bend the plank but rather to elevate the other end of the board by shifting the weight of the horse and rider further into the horse's hindquarters. The exact length of the neck, especially at the lower levels of show jumping, should be left to the horse's discretion. Our sole desire should be to produce a horse that maintains its balance when going to the jump.

It is my observation that horses learn to jump in three distinct phases where their eye-focus is concerned.

Phase one: In this phase, we are introducing horses that know nothing about jumping to various jumping problems. These problems should always have a generous ground line, as most green horses will look at the ground line in order to determine where to place their feet for the takeoff stride.

Phase two: By the use of gymnastics and related distances, we gradually adjust the ground line under the fence until the horse is able to successfully negotiate obstacles which, while solid in appearance, do present a vertical plane in front of the jump. This is an intermediate stage.

Phase three: As soon as the horse has matured enough to do small courses successfully, the rider should then go back and teach the horse to negotiate obstacles which contain no ground lines. This applies both to verticals and oxers, both in gymnastics and related distances, and as individual jumps. The height and spread should be lowered slightly as the horse will make a few mistakes, but as he lifts his eyes from the ground line through the center of the jump to the top of the rail, he will become both more accurate and more balanced in his approach.

THE EYES OF THE RIDER

IN order to jump fences well, you need to get your horse to the correct place in front of the jumps. This is a skill called "timing," which refers to a rider's ability to predict and influence the remaining increments of stride between any given point and the takeoff point. Most riders worry incessantly about their timing, yet fail to look at the next fence.

It is very difficult to know the remaining number of strides if you do not have a fixed point of reference. Looking beyond a jump places that jump in your peripheral vision, which is inaccurate when it comes to predicting whatever distance remains. Riders come to me with problems in their show jumping timing, and my answer is "If you want to improve your timing, look at the jump."

The rider looks at the top center of the first rail of a vertical. He looks at the top center of the first rail of an oxer. When the jump is either a double or triple bar the rider transfers his eyes to the back rail. For a very round oxer look at the back rail when the front rail is half the height or less than that of the back rail. This will place the horse's front feet closer to the front rail of the round oxer or triple bar, which is the desirable place for jumping a fence of this shape.

I feel the same way about timing my horse's stride that Garfield does about chocolate—I never met a stride I didn't like. Once you see what sort of stride you are going to get, you know what to do. If the horse is going to leave from a very long spot, make sure that you kick him off the ground and get up his neck as he makes

his effort. If you see that the horse is going to run under the fence, sit a bit more erect and keep hold of his head until he makes the effort with his front end to clear it. Try to make the same mistake that the horse makes. Your attitude should be that you are going to take the stride that you get and improve it.

Like the horse, the rider learns to use his eyes in a three-stage process, but he starts out looking straight ahead, not at the ground line.

Phase one: The novice rider is put in a two-point position with a neck strap, and made to look at the far wall or the horizon. This prevents the novice rider from anticipating the jumping motion or, even worse, looking down on top of the fence and toppling over on landing.

Phase two: At this point the rider is now told to look at the last fence in a line and then, when he gets close to the last jump, to look at the wall. This is the means by which instructors introduce the use of aids in controlling the direction of the horse to the next fence.

Phase three: This phase is the most misunderstood of the phases involved in teaching the rider to jump. As riders become competent, and handle courses involving changes of direction, in-and-outs, and related distances, they must change the focus of their eyes.

In phase three, the rider looks through the horse's ears at the top center of the rail of the next fence. He should keep his eyes fixed on this until the poll of the horse blocks out the rail. He then transfers his eyes to either the next obstacle, to the turn, or to a place in

---

OPPOSITE:

*T*HIS is how you should turn at speed over fences. Tim's weight is positioned over his inside stirrup; his outside elbow has relaxed, allowing the rein to come forward; his inside elbow has come back beginning the bending of the horse; his seat bones are still above the saddle; and his outside leg is slightly back. All of these subtle influences have caused the horse to wrap himself around Tim's leg and prepare for the next jump. The rider's eyes leave no doubt in anyone's mind where he is going next. Tim Grubb on Funny Face, Upperville Jumper Classic, Upperville, Virginia, 1993. TRICIA BOOKER

the arena where he is going to execute a transition. Be careful to understand the difference between what I am telling riders to do in phase three, and looking down. Looking down in the air causes riders to round their backs, to land with their shoulders in front of their stirrups, and to fall off. Looking at the jump increases the rider's confidence and improves his timing.

There is one more advanced phase, which involves timing by the rider that is so good that the horse thinks that he has done it himself. I have noticed that world-class riders look at the jump until they pick up their stride, usually five, six, or seven strides away. Then they ride in rhythm to this fence while they look at the following fence for their stride even before they have taken off over the first fence. There are probably twenty-five to fifty riders in the world at any given time who can do this. By the time you are that good, you will not worry about your timing. In the meantime, look at the jump.

EXERCISES TO DEVELOP TIMING

J HAVE several exercises to improve the rider's timing and to help the horse find the correct takeoff point. The first exercise occurs while working the horse in dressage at the canter. Occasionally pick a spot on the ground anywhere from five to ten strides away. Then, without altering the length of the horse's stride, look at that fixed point and try to predict when the horse is one stride away, two strides away, three strides away, and so on.

After a month or two of practice you will usually become quite accurate at predicting three strides. It takes years of intense jumping work before the rider's timing extends much beyond 45 feet. You should be patient in the approach, knowing that you need to be three strides or less away from the fence before you are going to be certain about how the horse will meet the jump, i.e., long, medium, or short.

The next exercise I use is to place a single rail on the ground and canter back and forth across it. This rail can also be used to improve the horse's flying changes, by working over the rail in a figure eight.

As I mentioned in the dressage section, flying changes on event horses should be done from a two-point in order not to confuse the horse between counter-canter and flying change during the dressage test. Using a rail on the ground, in addition, helps calm the approach of the horse. Many horses will overreact enormously to the placement of the rail at first. If the horse is overjumping, the rider should ride with a longer, looser rein rather than attempting to hold the horse on the ground by pulling on the reins.

If the horse continues to overjump the rail, put him on a 20-meter circle with the rail as part of that circle and let the horse stay on the circle until he starts to see the error of his ways.

Another exercise I use is to work the horse and rider through a related distance. Set up a vertical with a ground line, then measure 60 feet to a round oxer. Put both the vertical and the oxer at 3 feet 6 inches.

Canter over both fences, coming only from the vertical to the oxer. This exercise will produce either four long or five short strides. Practice going through the exercise in both four and five strides. Emphasize the striding that the horse finds more difficult. If he rushes, make him wait for five. If he is sluggish, make him leave out a stride, and so on. Remember to solve the distance in the first landing stride, not the last stride.

Imagine that you just did the exercise in five strides. Now, come again. This time, as you land over the vertical, say out loud, "land, one, two, three, four, five." Your voice should follow the strides of the horse. It should not increase in tempo as you get closer, or die away, but remain even and balanced. Do the exercise several times in both four and five strides, counting out loud each time. Occasionally, count the same number of strides after the oxer, to be sure that you keep your rhythm in the departure.

After you can maintain a steady pace in both four and five strides, discontinue counting. Repeat the same exercise but this time, in the air over the vertical, look at the oxer and say to yourself, "That's four long strides," or "That's five short strides." This will help calibrate your internal computer.

I've saved the best exercise for last. Set up a 3-foot-6-inch vertical, with a ground line on each side. Canter over the fence both ways a couple of times.

Pick a spot at least 100 feet before the fence. As you canter past that spot, start counting out loud. Keep counting until the horse leaves the ground at the vertical. Just as in the previous exercise, the important thing here is not the number of strides, but the regularity of the strides. Repeat this exercise on both leads and in both directions. Start counting in a slightly different spot each time, so you don't try and get the same number of strides each time. Concentrate instead on maintaining the regularity of the stride until the horse leaves the ground.

While you are counting out loud, look at the fence. Don't try to force a certain type of jump from your horse. Keep a steady, active stride as you approach the fence. About 50 feet away, you will get one of the following three sensations:

1. The fence seems to lean away from you. This means you are going to meet the fence on a long stride. Don't lean forward. Don't drop the reins. Just close your heels and ask the horse to move forward to the fence. You'll meet it on a comfortable forward stride.

2. The fence seems to lean toward you. This means you are going to meet the fence on a short stride. Open your hip angle, keep your leg and rein contact, and remind yourself not to drive at a short stride. If you wait for the horse to leave the ground, he will jump from a safe, conservative spot.

3. There is a "blank" inside you where the fence should be, or you "just feel nothing." For some reason, the subconscious signal we receive when we are going to meet a fence on a half-stride translates as a blank or empty feeling. Train yourself to add a stride whenever you get a blank signal. Sit up, close your reins and your legs, and keep the horse on the ground for an extra stride. Again, the horse will jump from a safe, conservative spot.

Timing is really very simple. Keep a regular stride, wait until you receive one of the three sensations described above, and help your horse according to the situation.

Or, as the old-timer said, "canter to the fence, and when there are no more strides left, let him leave the ground."

JUMPING AT THE TROT

*A*LTHOUGH the three-day event horse will earn his living jumping at the gallop, a great deal can be learned by jumping at the trot. The jumps should be lower, thus removing any apprehensions that you might have about jumping. In addition, lower fences enable you to preserve the soundness of the horse to a greater extent, thus allowing more practice. And finally, the pace is so much slower that you will be able to analyze what happens as the horse jumps.

The best way I've found to feel the horse jump is to set up a cavalletti exercise in the following manner. Place four rails on the ground, 4 feet 6 inches apart. Place a fifth rail 9 feet from the cavalletti on the ground between two standards. Now trot back and forth through this exercise until the horse moves in a steady regular rhythm. Maintain a central position over the horse, and post through the five cavalletti rails.

Notice that the horse takes five steps at the trot during this exercise—three steps in between each of the cavalletti rails and two steps during the 9-foot part of the exercise. The rhythm of these steps should not vary.

Raise the single rail on the ground to approximately 18 inches and approach at the posting trot, always approaching from the cavalletti end. Come through the exercise several times. You should feel that the horse has changed from a regular five-beat motion to one in which the fourth and fifth step happen almost simultaneously. At this point, take a break, and mentally review what happens at the point of takeoff.

Resume the exercise, attempting to maintain a posting motion all of the way into the fifth step. The trot is a two-beat motion, therefore posting has two beats. This means that you must feel the saddle again at either the fourth or the fifth beat of the exercise, thus placing your seat bones on the horse's back just as he pushes off. This contact will allow the horse's back to push you into the air and over the horse's shoulders at the required height above the saddle.

The most common bad habit of riders is to be ahead of the jumping motion. I think the reason for this is that riders separate their seat bones from the saddle both in the approach and at the moment of takeoff. For this reason I recommend that riders go to all of their fences in a light three-point contact. I noticed while riding in timber races that many of the best jockeys lowered their seat into the saddle during the last few strides. This maintained the security of their upper body, and allowed them to use their legs.

During the takeoff phase, be careful to follow the horse's mouth with the reins throughout, to maintain the security of the lower leg position, and to stay centrally balanced over the horse's body. The impression that the onlooker should get is that the horse jumps and the rider follows. There should not be any excess motion or strain, pushing or pulling on the part of the rider.

During the airborne phase of the jump you should concentrate on keeping your weight in the ankles and maintaining your knee grip. Remember that while the weight in the ankles keeps the lower leg at the girth, it is the knee grip which keeps you from falling off. Make sure that you can change the location of the grip as necessary. Some horses will need a fair amount of heel pressure off the ground to maintain their forward motion. Other horses will mistake this for a signal to rush and will follow their already unfortunate tendencies to increase their speed. For this sort of horse, grip more with your knees, and make sure you don't use your lower leg.

On landing, you should be in a light, three-point with the weight firmly in your knees and ankles and a light following contact with the reins. Do not snap back into a vertical position or topple forward until you are resting on your knuckles with your heels behind your hips. A horse usually lands in a fairly good balance. It is our loss of balance which causes trouble during the departure.

The position in the departure should be such that you are already balanced and prepared for the next fence, whether that fence is one, two, ten, or one hundred strides away from the present obstacle. A good rule of thumb is that the onlooker has the feeling you could jump another fence in the same speed, rhythm, and balance as the preceding fence.

Starting with the rail at 18 inches, gradually raise the rail in 3-inch increments until you can trot a vertical set at the height of your level, i.e., 3 feet 6 inches for Preliminary, 3 feet 9 inches for Intermediate, and 4 feet for Advanced. When the fence reaches 3 feet 9 inches move the standards and rail out 1 foot, so there are 10 feet from the last cavalletti rail on the ground to the fence.

Ride through this exercise in a steady rhythm. Keep a light, steady feel of the reins, and your legs closed but quiet. Don't push or pull on the reins. The cavalletti will provide the rhythm and ensure the correct takeoff spot. Just concentrate on being an intelligent passenger.

As the fence reaches 3 feet 6 inches you will start to feel the horse's head and neck actually move backward at the point of takeoff. This means the reins move backward an inch or so, and then move forward into the bascule. You are not pulling back on the reins but rather keeping a perfect following contact.

If you want to jump downhill verticals, or trekheners, you should master this motion of the reins. The bit serves the same role for the horse that the bamboo pole serves for the high-wire circus artist. Pushing or pulling won't help. A light steady contact will.

After you have jumped the exercise several times, you can let your horse off for the day or continue with more cavalletti exercises. When you lower the first jump after the cavalletti rails, remember to bring the standards and rail back from 10 feet to 9 feet.

ALTERING THE LENGTH OF
THE HORSE'S STRIDE

*M*ODERN course design requires the rider to demonstrate the horse's flexibility, both straight ahead and on curves. First practice altering the length of the horse's stride in straight lines. To do this you should understand the use of the reins in determining the shape that the horse takes in the air.

Speed alone is not the determining factor in the shape of a horse's jump—whether the arc becomes flat or very high and lofty. The horses that we see performing over 4-foot working hunter courses are ridden on a very soft, mostly loose rein. These horses take a lovely round shape in the air and probably come as close as any horse to the perfect bascule.

At the other end of the spectrum, hurdle horses take a very long, flat arc due to the extreme speed with which they approach their fences. However, you should also notice that the jockeys are definitely sitting against the horse's mouth to keep the head and neck up, the back flat, and to help the horse to land running.

Armed with this knowledge, you should be able to determine the shape of your horse's arc for whatever exercise is required of you. Most event riders have trouble shortening their horse's stride. It seems a bit contradictory at first to shorten the horse's stride by softening the reins in the air, but this is what is necessary. If you soften the reins in the air, the horse brings his head and neck around the fence more and lands closer to it. This has the effect of increasing the distance for the horse to approach the second, or succeeding, fence in an in-and-out or a line of jumps with related distances. The attempt should be made to jump into a short distance quietly, not to haul frantically on the reins once you arrive in the distance. Then, at the instant of landing, have the feeling that you are squeezing water out of a sponge. Land in balance and maintain the new, shorter, stride.

On the other hand, you must learn to lengthen the horse's stride, when necessary, by closing your legs, not by approaching at a faster rate of speed. At some point speed alone is going to cause the horse to knock the fence down, rather than allow him to cover the distance and still jump the fence with a nice round shape. The same principle exists for lengthening the show jumping stride as it does for lengthening the dressage stride. You should produce a longer stride but not a quicker stride.

The three-day event horse must be able to shorten and lengthen his stride quickly and easily with no loss of balance. Due to the excitability of the horses that most three-day riders deal with, we should probably teach the horse to wait for its stride first.

Set up this simple exercise over an 18-inch cross rail. Trot to the fence either way and jump it quietly until you and the horse are warmed up. Next, jump the fence and land quietly, taking special care not to topple forward or snap back in the saddle. As the horse canters away from the fence, ease into a three-point seat. Then drop your stirrups so that you cannot brace against anything and pull up in a straight line beyond the cross rail. The horse should come to a complete halt within approximately 50 feet. As you become more proficient at this exercise, this distance should shrink to 25 feet. Reassure your horse at the halt, pick up your stirrups, turn on the forehand or haunches, and trot over the cross rail the other way. Repeat this exercise until you can halt easily on a straight line.

During the first couple of repetitions you may need to be quite firm with a horse that is overly aggressive. Insist that the horse come to a halt. Once the horse finds out that you are serious about this exercise, he will usually begin to comply and pull up more readily. Make sure, during the pulling-up phase, that you do not squeeze your heels. Pull up by using your back and your reins, not your legs.

The horse does not need to be ridden with as much compression in jumping as it does in dressage. Usually if a horse is trotting or cantering, it has enough momentum to jump 3- to 4-foot fences without any additional assistance from your leg or rein. Be careful not to clash your aids during the jump. Simplify your signals to the horse. If you want to go, squeeze your legs and soften the reins. If you want to whoa, take the reins and soften the leg. But be careful not to drive your leg against your hand. Make the aids as clear and simple as possible to the horse.

Now that your horse is waiting for you, trot back and forth over the 18-inch cross rail, land, and have the feeling that you ease into a three-point position. The hands squeeze the reins as if you were squeezing water out of a sponge, and the horse should pull up quietly in a straight line without excess force on the part of the rider or any forms of resistance or tension on the part of the horse.

Now, set up two vertical fences, 2 feet high and 16 feet apart. Trot quietly into this exercise, land in a light three-point seat, and squeeze your fingers on the reins. Allow the horse to take one short stride at the canter and step out over the second 2-foot fence. If the horse complies with this exercise, trot back from the other direction. Repeat back and forth several times. If the horse shows signs of rushing, continue to pull up in a straight line, after the exercise.

It is entirely possible that you or the horse will panic at what appears to be an impossibly tight distance and bounce out. If this occurs, put a rail on the ground, exactly between the two fences, and repeat the exercise. After you are comfortable with this exercise, raise the fence in 3-inch increments to 3 feet, working in both directions. Remember, to increase the contact does not mean to pull backward on the reins.

You should have the feeling that you allow the horse to lean on the reins while jumping short combinations, not that you lean against the horse. Practice this exercise until the horse feels relaxed and you trust the horse to take a complete stride. Some horses that are very quick and aggressive need to practice exercises like this almost on a daily basis.

However, you must not practice one sort of exercise to the exclusion of another. The key to show jumping is that the horse remains flexible. This means he must be able both to go forward in his stride and to shorten his stride.

To teach your horse to lengthen his stride between fences, set up two square oxers 32 feet apart. Make them 2 feet 6 inches high and 3 feet wide, with ground lines on both sides of both oxers. Because of the width of the oxers, place a rail diagonally across the top of the oxer to keep your horse from thinking that the oxer is really a tight bounce. After you and the horse have jumped some single verticals and oxers, trot to this oxer combination. Remind yourself that the distance is quite long, and relax your elbows until the reins almost float. Try to achieve the same poised relaxation that the cavalletti-to-vertical exercise produced.

At the point of takeoff close your heels against the horse's sides and keep the reins soft. In the air, feel that you are attempting to push the horse across the first oxer and to land going faster than you took off. Be aggressive with your legs, especially in the first stride, and attempt to do this exercise in two strides. Let the reins float between the two oxers as long as the horse remains straight. Concentrate on riding vigorously forward with your lower leg. Throughout both this exercise and the 16-foot exercise above, make sure that you maintain a quiet, stable upper body position. All aids should occur from the legs or fingers, not from the shoulders or waist.

Your horse may chip in and add a third stride when first attempting this exercise. Persevere until the horse solves the problem and you learn the correct balance of aids to produce longer strides. If, after five or six attempts, the horse is still chipping in, shorten the distance between the oxers until the horse can produce the exercise in two strides. Then gradually lengthen the distance until the horse is covering 32 feet in two strides from the trot.

Practice this exercise until the horse just starts to anticipate, whether it takes two or ten repetitions to produce this anticipation. Then reverse, and come back through the exercise the other way. Again, practice the exercise until the horse just starts to anticipate and then discontinue the exercise. Later in the training, you can do this in two strides at the canter. The distance will then feel short.

It helps to work back and forth between these two exercises. This lengthening and shortening of the horse's stride seems to relax most horses. While it is true that the horse should concentrate on the exercise that he finds difficult, do not lose sight of the flexibility that is required of the horse's stride. The horse must lengthen and shorten his stride with equal facility.

Now that your horse can lengthen and shorten his stride, he should be taught to lengthen and shorten through in-and-outs or related distances. Start by building the same cavalletti-to-vertical as in the exercise described on page 157. Make the distance between the cavalletti 4 feet 6 inches, with 9 feet between the last cavalletti rail and a vertical with no ground line.

Raise the vertical in 3-inch increments until it reaches 3 feet 3 inches. Give the horse a break while you set up another vertical, 18 feet away from the first fence, again with no ground line.

Put the first fence at 2 feet 6 inches and the second fence at 3 feet. Start again.

When the horse has settled into the exercise, start to raise the second vertical in 3-inch increments. Keep raising the second fence until it is at least the maximum height of your competitive level. Continue to practice your basics while you let the horse jump the fence.

Stay in a light three-point seat between the first and second fence, and don't quicken your upper body movement as the fence gets larger. After four to six repetitions, let the horse take another break.

Leave the first fence at 2 feet 6 inches and return the second fence to 3 feet. Build a small square oxer 18 inches high and 3 feet wide, 20 feet from the second vertical. Place a third horizontal rail diagonally across the oxer, to keep the horse from bouncing into the oxer as we spread it.

TOP LEFT:

*H*ERE I am shown schooling Smitty through a long distance. Notice I am landing over a vertical stirrup leather; the rein contact is supportive; and my leg is close to my horse's sides. The seat bones should not return to the saddle until, as here, the horse's front feet have returned to the ground.   BRANT GAMMA

BOTTOM LEFT:

IT is not necessary to drive with your seat bones in order to extend the horse's stride at the canter. Because I had my legs on at the point of landing and maintained them, sending my horse into a steady rein, he has moved up, in quite a long distance, to a low flat spread. A bit too much inclination of my upper body.   BRANT GAMMA

ABOVE:

MY horse is still on my reins, even though I have asked him to extend his stride. This accounts for the coiled sensation you get when looking at this horse in the air. The lower leg should be slightly more forward. The author on General Lion, Fox Covert Farm, Upperville, Virginia, 1993.   BRANT GAMMA

The distance will be long between the second fence and the oxer. Solve the problem the same way you did in the 32-foot oxer-to-oxer exercise. At the takeoff point in front of the second fence, close your heels. Ask your horse to land going forward to the oxer and don't touch the reins as long as your horse is straight.

Repeat this exercise until your horse understands the distance. Then spread the back rail of the oxer in 18-inch increments until the oxer is between 5 and 6 feet wide. Don't raise the oxer. Just spread it, replacing the diagonal third rail every time you move the back rail. Let your horse repeat the maximum spread you plan to jump two or three times, then give him another short break.

Now move the back rail of the oxer in to create a 4-foot spread, and then build another 3-foot vertical 19 feet from the oxer. You should now have four fences in a row—vertical at 2 feet 6 inches, 18 feet to a vertical at 3 feet, 20 feet to an oxer 18 inches by 4 feet wide, and 19 feet to a new vertical at 3 feet.

The rhythm of this exercise has now become quite complex, requiring your horse to come in at a balanced, steady pace, then to explode over the oxer, and finally to shorten his stride to handle the 19-foot distance. The last element will not seem too close at first, which is a good thing. You don't want to trap your horse but rather to educate him. However, as you raise the last rail, again in 3-inch increments, the distance will come to feel close indeed. If your horse hangs or knocks down the last rail, lower it, put a ground line 18 inches from the vertical, and build it up again. The last rail should eventually reach 4 feet.

If you study the requirements of the exercise in terms of their effect on the horse's stride, you will find that they go: balance, lengthen, shorten. Sounds just like a classical dressage movement, doesn't it? If you can do this exercise smoothly, at the height of your competitive level, you're riding pretty well. Eventually the capable Advanced three-day event horse should come through this exercise at 3 feet 6 inches, 4 feet, 18 inches by 5 feet, and 4 feet. Remember to check the distance from the back oxer rail to the last vertical.

Obviously, this is a strenuous workout for any horse. He should have been jumping for at least thirty days before attempting this exercise, and even then, not at the maximum heights or spreads right away.

COMMON PROBLEMS IN JUMPING

RUSHING

*T*HERE are several problems in the horse's technique that are common to training jumpers. Probably the most usual bad habit of event horses is rushing. Although this can be an uncomfortable sensation for you, a certain amount of aggression on the part of the horse is necessary if it is going to be a successful three-day event horse.

Because it is so important that a three-day event horse jump whatever we put in front of him, I rarely pull up in front of an obstacle. We have to find a way to discipline the horse, yet awaken his initiative at the same time.

Rather than attempting to dominate the horse, you should deal with rushing in a cheerful manner, viewing it as a positive trait. The best way that I have found to get a horse to balance and stop rushing is to jump from the trot with fences in a straight line and a rail on the ground in between each fence. Thus, if you have 18 feet between a vertical and an oxer, there would be a rail on the ground 9 feet after the vertical. This causes the horse to think about where he is going to place his feet, and to pause slightly at the takeoff.

At the same time, you should rethink the use of the reins. Attempt to float the reins to the horse's mouth rather than pulling back on the reins in the air over the jump. Pulling back will cause the horse to continue to rush for self-preservation or, indeed, get worse. The rail on the ground can be repeated for subsequent jumps if you are jumping more than two fences in a row.

Another beneficial exercise is to have a ground man walk in front of the horse as the horse is six or eight steps at the trot before the first fence. Again, this will confuse the horse slightly and cause him to pause. Any time the horse pauses, you should immediately soften the reins and lower the hands so that the horse keeps himself between your leg and the fence rather than between your leg and your hand.

Some trainers will raise fences until the horse starts to slow down, but I do not regard this as an acceptable training practice. Basically, what you are doing is injecting an element of fear into the training equation, attempting to terrify the horse into slowing down. The line between this practice and teaching the horse to refuse is too fine for my liking. I am much more inclined to take the long way around and do the job right the first time rather than having to do it over later on.

Occasionally a horse will rush so badly when jumping in straight lines that it will bounce a one-stride combination or take one enormous long stride and one violent short stride in a two-stride combination. This should be dealt with by jumping on looser reins, and by placing poles on the ground, which will dictate to the horse where he should place his feet, and, therefore, how many strides he should take.

STOPPING

*I*F the horse does refuse, for whatever reason, you must immediately punish him. Our theory in training horses is that we get them to jump in spite of anything we do, rather than because of everything that we do. You might say to yourself, "I dropped the horse, and, therefore, he stopped." But the lesson to the horse must be, "You stopped, therefore, you get punished." Then approach the fence again, attempting to ride correctly this time.

In any case, the horse must come to the jump convinced that it is his responsibility to find a way over it. He should not rely on you. There is no sense in galloping down to a telephone pole cemented in the ground with a horse that is waiting to be told what to do with his feet. I never wanted a horse that I had to be good enough to ride. I wanted a horse that jumped despite anything I did, not because of everything I did.

The most important thing of all is extravagant praise both by patting and by use of the voice after the horse successfully negotiates the obstacle. We train our horses using reward and punishment. We have to make sure that we are willing to use punishment sparingly and at the correct time. We must be prepared to reward often, and we must be satisfied with small steps of progress. If you can improve your horse only 1 percent a day, you will get where you want to go in the long run. If you are determined to enforce major changes in the horse's behavior in a short period of time, you're probably going to end up disappointed.

DRIFTING

*A*NOTHER common habit of horses is drifting—jumping to the side—when jumping in straight lines, or jumping toward the corner of the fence. Horses learn to do this for several reasons. They may be unsound; they may have a rider who depends more on one rein than the other for balance; the rider may lean to one side more than another; or finally, the horse may have done a great deal of jumping in straight lines and have learned that there is more distance on the diagonal between two fences than there is in a straight line.

First of all, ensure that you are part of the solution and not part of the problem. Jump through the exercise on loose reins several times. Make sure that the horse is swerving to the side for some reason not connected with your position. If the horse continues to jump to the side, put up a half cross rail just behind the horizontal rail. This rail should rest on top of the standard and not be fixed in a cup, and it should be behind the horizontal rail, not in front, for safety reasons. For example, if the horse jumps to the right, the rail should rise from the center of the horizontal rail to the top of the right standard. There are other means of correcting horses that drift but this is the most efficient way that I have found.

JUMPING AT THE CANTER

*E*ARLY in the conditioning schedule the best way of reintroducing an experienced horse to jumping at the canter is by jumping on curves. When jumping two or more fences on related curves you should keep several things in mind. First of all, the turn should be made by use of the open leading rein and the outside neck or bearing rein, not by leaning back and frantically pulling on the

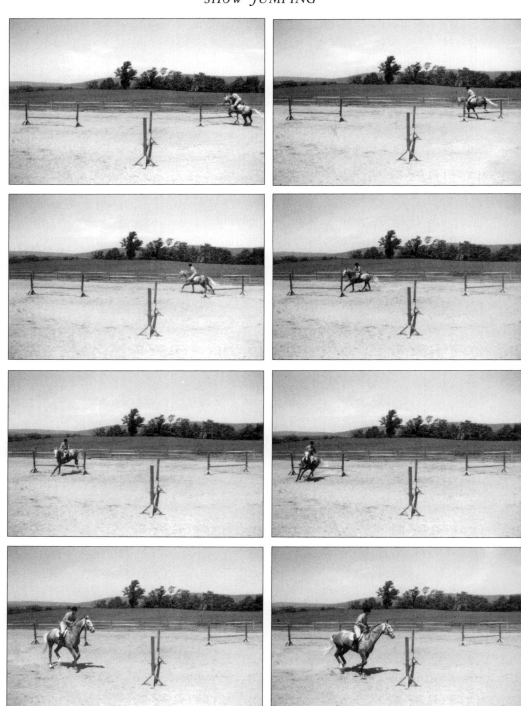

COMPARE this series with the photographs of Packy MacGaughan on Tanzer (page 172) and Tim Grubb on Funny Face (page 152), and also with Course 9 in Appendix III. This is an exercise I use to teach young horses to turn quickly and easily. Turn your horse by landing over your inside knee. Open your inside rein and bring your outside rein against the neck. Push your horse into the curve with your outside leg—don't try to pull him around with the inside rein. Whatever you are trying to teach your horse will come easier if you ride with your legs.

I look across the turn to the next fence, and keep my eyes on the rail until it goes out of sight, then I look to the next rail, and so on. Treat the rails as something in the way of your rhythm, rather than as something to be jumped. When you have an option, let the horse take another stride. You should never be ashamed to jump small fences. You can jump more of them, and you can learn from your mistakes, rather than shaking your, and your horse's, confidence. The author on General Lion, Fox Covert Farm, Upperville, Virginia, 1993.   BRANT GAMMA

I LIKE for training to be progressive and systematic. Once your horse has mastered the exercise shown for Course Nine in Appendix III, you can ask him to go the same way in the competition arena. Packy is going to land on the left lead and go directly to the next fence for two reasons—he trained his horse correctly and he used the correct aids (inside leg at the girth, outside leg behind the girth, open rein to the inside, and outside neck rein). Packy's weight is slightly over his inside knee and his eyes are on the next fence. Technique like this will produce clear rounds for your country in international arenas. Packy MacGaughan on Tanzer, Indianapolis Pan-Am Games, 1987.   KARL LECK

inside rein. Your inside leg should remain at the girth. You should attempt to land slightly above the inside knee. The outside leg is there to control the hindquarters and to maintain the bending of the horse's body, not only in the approach to the jump but in the air over the jump. When jumping on curves, the horse should continue the curve in the air.

The next thing to remember is that your eyes must always be looking at the next element. If you look away from the next jump, you will lose a priceless opportunity to pick up your rhythm and your timing.

Once you have become adept at jumping on curves, you should rarely get a bad stride. The reason for this is that you should use the curve of your approach to adjust your stride. By opening one rein or the other, you can have a major effect on the takeoff point without disturbing your horse's stride or balance.

To practice this, put two rails on the ground at right angles to each other, with 24 inches from the end of one rail to the end of the other. Canter over these two rails until you can turn in either two, three, or four strides. This will teach you how to use the curve to effect your takeoff. Now make the rails small vertical jumps and repeat.

As a general comment, the ability of the horse to accept contact in the air over a fence is always going to be one stage behind that ability on the flat. As the dressage improves, the hocks will engage and the neck will shorten and elevate. As the jumping improves, the same process will occur, but it will occur later than in dressage. This is due to the tension that usually arises in both rider and horse when the subject of jumping comes up.

ANALYZING COURSES

*W*HEN analyzing a show jumping course, there are four elements of difficulty. The course designer considers (1) the height of the jumps, (2) the spread, (3) the striding between jumps, and (4) the length of the track of the course in order to make it easy or hard to make the time. In terms of three-day eventing, because the height and the spread of obstacles on the show jumping course

THE difference between normal show jumping and jumping on the third day of a three-day event is the degree of fatigue in the three-day event horse. You have to let your horse lean on you, and help him with stronger than normal legs and reins. Here Bea has a good hold of her horse's head and a strong leg as she helps her horse over the fence. The excellence of her basic jumping technique shows up under the pressure of trying to jump a clean round. Bea diGrazia on Irish Trick, Badminton, 1977. FINDLAY DAVIDSON

are so strictly regulated, they really do not form part of the problem. The problem is more in the striding between elements and occasionally, at the higher levels, by the way that the course has been measured.

You need to control the horse's balance, his speed, his direction, and the length of his stride. Most of these requirements can be controlled by using one word—dressage. We have to make the horse flexible in our work on the flat so that, when he comes to the jumping phase, he is more easily controlled and directed in his efforts to get us around the course. All exercises over jumps, which can improve the horse and rider's performance, are, in effect, rehearsals before the competition. After you have been to one or two horse trials at the start of the season, you should have a fairly good idea of what is difficult and what is easy about your horse in the show jumping phase. Then the question becomes, how can I improve this horse?

The basic approach to training the horse in the show jumping phase should be to proceed from the simple to the complex. In theory the horse should never be asked to do anything in competition that it has not practiced at home. Analyze various problems that your horse presents, such as difficulty in turning to one side or another, difficulty in shortening the stride after jumping a spread, and so on. Once difficulties have been identified, develop exercises which, when practiced in miniature, will teach the horse to handle the problem more easily. Here, as in all other aspects of riding, your idea should be to proceed from the simple to the complex, from the low to the large.

WALKING THE COURSE

*Y*OU can beat most of your competition before the first rider steps in the ring. This will happen in two ways. First of all, most riders will content themselves with learning the way between fences. You must analyze the show jumping course, not just in an effort to find out where fences number one, two, three are but also to analyze where the easy and the difficult parts of the course are located. Many times just a little preparation on a turn or a slight tap on the horse's shoulder entering a long distance will be sufficient to solve the problem. But if you sit there fat, dumb, and happy, you're going to become a statistic rather than a winner.

The second mistake many riders make is not relating the course to their own horse's strengths and weaknesses. Analyze the course, not just in terms of where the track goes, and, indeed, not just in terms of where the difficult and easy parts are, but what will be difficult or easy for your horse. If it is a good course design, there will be problem areas that will test your control over your horse and, the designer hopes, provide a balanced result at the end of the competition. But many times horses will handle certain elements of a course far more easily than a course designer might like. Planning ahead will increase your chances of being in that group.

PACING DISTANCES BETWEEN ELEMENTS

*W*HEN pacing the distance, you should consider fences related that are 75 feet or less apart. It is essential that you know the relationship between jumps in terms of the striding. The distance between two jumps will determine the number of strides that the horse will take in its approach to the second fence and, many times, will determine the rider's attitude toward the first fence. I've mentioned before that related distances are solved in the approach to the first element and on landing after the first element, rather than in the approach to the second. But all of this presupposes that the rider has recognized the problem.

There are enough variables in jumping horses already. Do not introduce more by pacing with an uneven stride. Practice the following exercise. Take five markers and a measuring wheel or measuring tape. Set one marker at the end of the ring or area where you can measure off an extended distance. Then put a marker at the normal distance intervals. That is, 24 feet, 36 feet, 48 feet, and 60 feet. You now have four known, measured distances. It is up to you to adjust your stride so that you can pace, using 3-foot strides, with a high degree of accuracy. After some practice, you should be able to pace 60 feet and arrive within 6 inches one way or the other.

This may seem overly mechanical, but I can assure you when you pace a downhill vertical combination in deep mud, it makes a big difference that you know whether it is 21, 24, or 27 feet between elements because that will determine, to a great extent, your success or failure. It's not just a ribbon, it's your neck. Know what you are doing and then do it.

THE WARM-UP

*T*HE first thing you should know about the three-day event show jumping test is that your horse is going to feel different. If this is your first three-day event, you may be taken aback by the difference in the way your horse feels as opposed to the way it feels during horse trials. Many times horses which are easy to control in one-day events become intoxicated after the steeplechase and cross-country phase. Other horses may come out stiff and sore from their exertions and not be as elastic as you might expect.

There's nothing to do except make sure that the horse receives a good preparation and ride the horse the way he actually presents himself for the show jumping phase, not as you might wish. There is nothing wrong with these changes per se. What is wrong with it is that sometimes a rider gets a mental block and tries to ride the horse that he used to have and not the horse that he is dealing with at present.

Regardless of whether the horse is overly exuberant or somewhat sleepy, be convinced of one thing: the horse must be ridden on a much firmer contact than is normally the case. If the horse is exuberant, he is going to need the reins to restrain him. If he is tired, he is going to need extra help from you to get his forehand off the ground in time to clear the rails.

Don't be surprised by the changes in the horse before the show jumping in horse trials, either. Many horse trials are held in different configurations. By that, I mean that the show jumping sometimes follows the dressage and sometimes follows the cross-country. Obviously, horses will be different using one type of schedule rather than another. This is an excellent opportunity to find out how your horse is going to ride once you get him to a three-day event. If you listen carefully to the horse during the preparation competitions, there should not be many surprises left once you get to the three-day event. Horse trials should always be viewed as a means of training and preparation rather than as a competitive end in themselves.

During the warm-up take into consideration the physical condition of the horse. After the exertions of the speed and endurance day, a horse does not need a great deal of jumping. Ten minutes of trot, three or four minutes of canter, two cross rails, cantering a couple of low jumps, cantering a higher vertical, and cantering a medium-sized oxer are about all the horse needs before he goes in.

I have never had much luck with "bumping" three-day event horses (that is, letting them hit a rail on purpose). Three-day event horses probably have too high a fear threshold and too high a pain threshold. They're not afraid, and it doesn't bother them to hit something. So they don't react the same way that show jumping horses do to bumping a fence. I think that the emphasis should be on giving your horse an accurate, smooth, steady stride and arriving at the jumps in balance. Given that type of approach you will probably jump as many clean rounds as any other rider.

Any of the more esoteric methods such as tack rails, wires, bamboo poles, and the like have never formed a very big part of my training methods at home and I disapprove of them for the most part. Concentrate on making your horse generous, keeping him balanced, and giving him the best possible ride, and you will be successful.

This does not mean that, for example, if your horse has difficulty with long distances, you should not gallop to a couple of oxers with a bit of spread on them in the schooling ring. If your horse is a bit slow in front, possibly you should emphasize a couple of verticals at the height of your division. But one or two timely reminders is all that you should provide. Endless drilling before the show jumping usually leads to fatigue, which leads to knockdowns and lost ribbons. If you know your horse and you analyze the course in the terms that we have described, and you warm your horse up keeping these things in mind, the course itself should be the natural culmination to the training process, not some horrifying experience for horse and rider.

WHEN your horse leaves the ground, you start preparing for the next fence. Spread water jumps are quite rare in three-day event show jumping situations. When you encounter them they should be jumped as a triple bar, not as an open ditch. I am preparing to land and shorten Paddy's stride in preparation for a vertical on a related distance a few strides away. The author on Mr. and Mrs. Richard Thompson's Castlewellan, Burghley, Stamford, Lincs, England, 1983. EQUESTRIAN SERVICES THORNEY

*Y*OU gallop more than you jump when you are on course. Make sure that when you land over a jump, you land galloping in this shape—low hands, body placed over the withers, leg underneath you. If you're really clever, you can be looking at your watch at the same time. Karen Lende on Mr. Richard Thompson's Mr. Maxwell, Badminton, 1992. BRANT GAMMA

7

Conditioning

ONE of the most frequent questions I am called on to answer is "How much work should I give my horse before a three-day event?" There are as many answers to this as there are horses getting ready for three-day events and trainers training them. What I intend to do in this chapter is show you the format that has worked for me and give you some guidelines to help you develop your own system for training horses.

The first thing you must do when training three-day event horses is to set your priorities. My priorities are, always, in the following order:

1. *Soundness.* It is possible to take a horse that is feeling well, but is short one or two gallops, to a three-day event and complete the course successfully with no ill effects. However, if the horse is not sound, you are not going to be able to take part in the competition at all. All of your scheduling, all of your work, must be aimed at producing a sound, fit horse and not just a fit horse.

2. *Fit.* The horse must be fit to do the test involved on the speed and endurance day. This means that his lungs must be

prepared for the stress of the steeplechase phase as well as for the endurance aspect of the cross-country section. The level of fitness required will vary according to the level of difficulty. To a certain extent, you must find out for yourself how much work the horse needs to produce that particular horse fit and ready to run.

3. *Technical skills.* After we have made sure that the horse is sound and fit, then we can schedule the preparation of the horse's technical skills, i.e., its dressage, its cross-country, its show jumping, and its steeplechase phase. Remember that the horse can be a bit fresh in dressage and still do well. However, if you emphasize dressage to the exclusion of all else, you will win the first day and then vanish. One of the great satisfactions in training three-day event horses is to arrive at the event with all your skills equally and adequately prepared.

SCHEDULES AND DIARIES

*U*SE two tools to plan and organize your horse's training. The first of these is a schedule. This is a projection of what sort of work, how often, how much, and what type you intend to give the horse over, roughly, the next thirty days.

The second tool is to maintain a diary. By diary I do not mean a "Dear Diary, my horse was terrible today" sort of operation, but rather a fairly cut and dried listing of the physical exercise that the horse engaged in that day. Many times the schedule and the diary will differ. The schedule tells you what you're going to do next; the diary tells you what you've already done. Keep your diaries. They will become an invaluable reference source after you collect a few.

Be careful to use the schedule to help you train the horse. Do not let the schedule train you. For example, a horse that has done a gallop of medium severity yesterday may have been scheduled for a dressage lesson today. When the horse comes out, obviously muscle sore and slightly jaded, the best thing you can do is to throw the schedule over your shoulder and give the horse a day off. Check to make sure that his legs have come to no injury, and turn him out or hand-walk him for that day. Most of the time the horse will be back to himself the following day and you can continue the schedule as if nothing had happened, taking in rotation whatever activity you had planned for that day. The schedule is strictly a guideline, not a rule.

THE INTERVAL SYSTEM

$\mathcal{M}$OST people these days use some form of interval system to prepare their horses for three-day events. Before you decide exactly what form of interval system to use, decide on what rotation to use. By rotation, I mean the sequence of the activities of your horse during the training cycle. A schedule that goes dressage, jump, dressage, jump makes more sense than a schedule that goes jump, jump, dressage, jump, jump. In deciding on the rotation you make a major decision and one that should not be taken lightly, for you are determining the success or failure of the horse.

There are two basic rotations to be used. Note that neither one of them provides for a day off during the training cycle. Usually I handle this by scheduling a day off when it makes sense in the horse's preparation. That is, I may plan to have a day off and an easy day for the two days following a horse trials. I may give the horse a day off after a particularly hard work and I will look for free times during the schedule, when I feel that the horse may have done a bit too much work, in order to let him off and allow his body to refresh itself.

The two different rotations that can be used are four-day or five-day cycles. The first of these is a four-day rotation. A four-day rotation looks like this: Day 1: dressage; Day 2: show jumping; Day 3: dressage; Day 4: canter; Day 5: repeat Day 1.

A five-day rotation looks like this. Day 1: hack and dressage; Day 2: hack and show jumping; Day 3: hack and dressage; Day 4: canter/gallop; Day 5: long hack; Day 6: repeat Day 1. This cycle is more suitable for three-day event horses; note the hack that is included on four out of five days of the cycle. If your horse is wild, hack him first. If he is dopey, hack him after his technical work.

The four-day rotation is more suitable for lower level horses, novice riders who forget how to ride if they miss a day, or for young horses that forget all of their technical work if they are given a day off. The four-day rotation is not as applicable once the canter starts to become a gallop. Because of the emphasis on soundness, the most strenuous day in my schedule is always followed by the easiest day. This gives the horse's system an extra day to recover from the stress of the gallop.

Horses are very prone to injury when working on rough, hard footing. You will shorten the competitive career of your horse greatly if you do not take particular care with the footing for the gallops. If your training area does not provide suitable terrain, you must take the trouble to ship to a local racehorse track. It is better for your horse to be sound but a bit bored by going in circles than to have him in a wonderful, cheerful mood but lame. Certainly a stopwatch will come in handy at first, but later on you must be able to sense your pace rather than mechanically look at a watch. The watch is there as a crutch. But sooner or later, you should throw your crutches away and ride by your feel.

GUIDELINES TO FITNESS

J USUALLY like the horse to do a great deal of slow cantering before he starts any speed work. I think it takes a long time for the horse's system to toughen and adapt. Once you build a broad enough base, you can then start to sharpen the horse by decreasing the distance and increasing the speed. Speed should be used late in the set and, when two sets are used, the speed in the second set should be greater than that in the first.

Structuring the work in this way also has a definite tendency to sharpen the horse's attitude toward his dressage and show jumping. Take that into account during the days following a sharp gallop. One of the problems in preparing a three-day event horse is to bring him to peak fitness but with all three disciplines in balance. Having a horse almost racehorse fit and yet calm, supple, and obedient in the dressage are almost diametrically opposed requirements. I like the horse to do "three sixes" on at least three separate occasions before starting any speed work. I want the horse, before its first horse trials, to have cantered "three sixes" twice and have had a

*W*HEN you're galloping at the biggest cross-country jump in the world, you can't hold back. Jim has maintained his classical position although he is, obviously, urging Rosie (Easter Parade) forward to Centaur's Leap. The balance of the horse is maintained by the straight line from the elbow to the horse's bit. The closing of the lower leg leaves no doubt what Jim wants to happen here. Jim Graham on Easter Parade, Burghley CCIO, Stamford, Lincs, England, 1993. EQUESTRIAN SERVICES THORNEY

A SUPERBLY balanced takeoff over an enormous ditch and hedge. Jim has maintained the pressure of his lower leg and has, very correctly, pressed the horse into a steady contact. Some riders have a tendency to push the reins at their horse, trying to get it to jump. That will cause you nothing but trouble. Keep the horse compressed, and allow that energy to create the horse's jump. Look at the similarity between Jim's rein contact here and in the photo on page 93. Both riders are going forward with their bodies but maintaining their contact. Jim Graham on Easter Parade, Burghley, Stamford, Lincs, England, 1993. EQUESTRIAN SERVICES THORNEY

*H*AVING galloped freely forward to a big fence and supported his horse off the ground, all Jim has to do now is fold up and enjoy the ride. The upper body placement is exactly where you would like to see it, poised in the middle of the horse, with the seat off the saddle and the lower legs close to the girth—an excellent example of jumping an enormous fence with a classical position and aids. Although things are going well, I like the slightly defensive feel of this photo. Jim Graham on Easter Parade, Burghley CCIO, Stamford, Lincs, England, 1993. EQUESTRIAN SERVICES THORNEY

cross-country school at 400 to 450 meters a minute over roughly 1,600 meters before going to his first horse trial of the season.

At the lower levels, horses that can slow canter twice the distance of their course are probably fit enough to go around a horse trials course quietly. Due to the increased speed at the Intermediate and Advanced levels, the horse should do more conditioning work before competing at those levels.

THIRTY-DAY SCHEDULING

THE first thing to do when planning a schedule for your horse is to take a blank sheet of paper. Work backward for thirty days from the next event where you intend to compete. Then, fill in special days, such as combined tests and schooling days. If you have any personal commitments that will take you away from your horse for a day or so, now is the time to plan for them, so that you can keep the horse improving even when you are not around.

Then decide upon the rotation that you are going to use. If your horse is competing at the Training and Preliminary horse trials level, you can quite safely use a four-day rotation. If your horse is competing at Intermediate or Advanced horse trials or preparing for a three-day event, he should be using a five-day rotation. This gives him a break after the exertions of a more strenuous gallop day.

Having decided on your rotation and filled in the special days, work backward from the event and fill in the blank days. When completed, this is your schedule for the next month. This is a guideline and not a rule, but it will help you organize your work.

I usually schedule only for about thirty days in advance. Anything more than that is really a pipe dream where horses are concerned. There are too many instances of thrown shoes, mild overreaches, coughs, and so on, that cause a horse to miss a few days of work. You're better off to schedule in shorter, more realistic, time frames.

After you have competed at a horse trials, compare the schedule with your diary, and with your results at the horse trials. For example, if you win the dressage, go clean and fast around the cross-country, but knock down every show jumping rail, it's fairly obvious what is going to happen during the next training period. You

ONCE you have mastered the exercises illustrated on pages 162 and 163, your horse will know how to take this shape. Derek is, obviously, traveling at a high rate of speed and has asked his horse off a very long stride. Once he gets it, all he needs to do is follow and continue to support with his legs and reins. Derek diGrazia on Sasquatch, owned by Mrs. Craig Christensen, World Championships, Gawler, Australia, 1986. GOWER PHOTOS

certainly should emphasize show jumping in the schedule that you will formulate as you prepare for the next competition. On the other hand, if the horse wins the dressage but blows up around the cross-country, taking twenty-five to thirty minutes to recover after the cross-country phase, he has not been getting enough work. You need to increase his physical fitness before the next time out at this level.

PLANNING YOUR GALLOPS

*P*lan your gallops to produce the horse in peak condition at the three-day event. This means two things. It means the horse does not have to be racing fit for the first horse trial of the season and that the horse trials themselves should be included as part of the conditioning work. I do not think that horses should be put under the same sort of pressure to make the time at their first event of the spring that they should be put under later.

Use the same procedure that you do for the overall schedule. That is to work backward. You should decide what the last work before the three-day event should be and then plan five days before that for a work that leads up to your last work. Then, an additional five days back, you should have a work which, again, is slightly slower and slightly shorter than the one which will follow it, and so on back up the schedule.

Be sure to keep your schedules, as they will form an excellent reference point as you continue to prepare horses for three-day events. If carefully prepared and intelligently ridden, a CCI* is well within the capabilities of most horses and riders, and the rewards for your preparation and effort are beyond anything available to you in any other horse sport.

It is only natural to be unsure of yourself if you are new to the sport. Just follow the techniques outlined here, organize your daily work in a sensible fashion, and remember that your horse is in your care and, in a manner of speaking, has the final word. All you have to do to succeed is *decide* to succeed.

WHEN your horse takes a cut at a fence, you need a safety seat. Bea is showing you how to do it here, putting her lower leg forward and just starting to let the reins slide through her open fingers. There is no doubt that when the horse lands, Bea will be placed exactly in the middle of her horse; and Bea's eyes tell you that she will land galloping to the next fence. Bea diGrazia on Suzy D, RamTap, Fresno, California, 1986.

8

Putting It All Together

ONCE you have applied all of the material contained in the preceding chapters, it's time for the fun part. Putting it all together at a three-day event is what your hard work and effort are aimed toward. Riders have a tendency to self-destruct once they get to a three-day event. Don't let this happen to you. By now you have an accurate idea of your horse's capabilities. You have, obviously, qualified for the three-day event or the rules would not allow you to participate. You have probably completed several horse trials successfully within the last sixty days. And, if you have applied one of the conditioning schedules that is listed in Appendix II, you can be sure that your horse is fairly fit. Concentrate on arriving at the three-day event determined to display your horse to his best abilities, rather than just win a ribbon.

The first thing to do when arriving on the grounds is to get the horse settled in to his stall. If you are at an FEI event, you have to go through an In-Barn Examination by one of the official veterinarians. Once you have taken care of this, go to the Secretary's stand and get your competitor's packet. This should include your number, which will possibly give you a chance to estimate your start time for the dressage phase.

Everything you do from the time of your arrival on the grounds should be aimed at producing your horse in the best possible mental and physical condition as you turn down the center line of the dressage arena. One of the places that riders beat themselves is by overpreparing their horses' dressage. If you get to the grounds on a

ONE of the hardest lessons to learn is not to overjump your steeple-chase fences in a three-day event. Wash is riding his horse as economically as possible, not asking for big fences but trying to get Taxi to jump out of stride. The expression on Wash's face tells you that he is in a team event and is utterly focused on the task at hand. Wash Bishop on Taxi, Alternate Olympics, Fontainebleau, France, 1980. FINDLAY DAVIDSON

Tuesday, you do not want your horse to go his best on Wednesday. You want to prepare him in such a fashion that he is at his best on Friday for his dressage time. For most horses this means extra time in the saddle, but you do not want to work your horse endlessly. Many horses, especially Thoroughbred types, benefit from hacking out and wandering around the grounds on a loose rein—"taking your nerves for a walk."

Discuss your warm-up plans with your groom. Make sure that he knows when you want the horse to go out and what tack you want on it.

I disapprove of jumping the horse once you get to the grounds. There is very little that you will be able to teach him; you are taking a slight risk in jumping; and there is no chance that your horse has forgotten how to jump since your last show jumping school or competition horse trials. I have had horses that were better in their dressage after show jumping, but they were definitely in the minority. Most horses equate "jump" with "gallop" and "gallop" with excitement. Excitement does not mix with dressage very well. Concentrate on keeping your horse in a mellow, settled frame of mind, rather than worrying if you can still jump a three-foot-six-inch post-and-rail.

WALKING AND RIDING THE COURSE

*Y*OU should walk Phase D, the cross-country course, at least three times before competing. The first time is to learn your way around and be sure that you can find your way from one jump to the next. During the first or the second course walk, use a meter wheel. Many times cross-country courses are longer or shorter than their published distance. This is an essential item of information for you. Know the published distance of the course, and note the quarter, half, and three-quarter markers as you reach them. When you reach the end of the course, compare the distance you get by measuring where you intend to ride with the published distance. Don't be surprised if you find one or two hundred meters' variation either way.

This is invaluable knowledge. It means that the course is going to ride faster or slower than the published distance. You are not required to share this information with the Technical Delegate or the organizers, and it should be viewed as an edge on the competition. It is the Technical Delegate's and course designer's responsibility to measure the course accurately. It's your job to get around the course the best way you can, taking the least amount out of your horse as possible so that he can compete another day.

Over long courses (6,000 meters or more) after I have measured the course, I set my wheel back to zero at the finish line. Then I measure backward on the course until I know where the "one minute" and "two minutes from home" markers are. For example, if you are competing at the Intermediate level and the speed is 550 meters per minute, you would wheel back 550 meters and then 1,100 meters to establish your one minute and two minutes from home markers. These are excellent items of information to have if you are unsure about whether to continue to try to make the time or to canter home quietly and accept some time faults.

The second walk will probably take you the longest, as it is now that you will decide exactly where you intend to jump each fence, especially the combination and option fences.

During this course walk, look back between fences. This will sometimes cause you to adjust your line in approaching the next jump. You should also decide what you are going to do if you have trouble. If you have a refusal in a combination, you should not lose additional time and get penalized any more than is necessary. Plan your next approach. Many times there is an easier, but slower, way out of a combination. If you have had a refusal at one element, you may be much better off to go the long route and get through the combination. Don't get in trouble and then try to make it up. Have alternate routes planned in your mind. It is a good idea to walk around with a coach or a more experienced rider, or at least to seek the advice of riders more experienced than you, to be sure you are jumping the fences at the correct speed and on the correct line.

The third time you should walk alone early in the morning of the day of the competition. At this point you should make a "film" in your mind of exactly how the course looks to you when no one else is on it. Look at the next fence as you walk toward it, and visualize how you plan to ride if everything is going well.

As the competition gets closer, you should be amused at the

obvious nerves that appear in some of your fellow competitors. Complaints about the footing, the dangerous design of some perfectly jumpable obstacle, or whatever, are going to abound. Try to ignore them. If you have made a good plan, stick to it.

Don't change your attitude because of a change in the conditions. For example, most riders have a tendency to look out the motel room window at six o'clock in the morning and say, "Ugh! It's raining. I'm not going to have fun today." Of course, their attitude is going to carry over to their horse and then to their performance. I happen to like duck hunting, so I am accustomed to being exposed to extreme weather conditions. I used to look out the window at the rain or wind, snow, whatever, and say to myself, "Oh boy! I'm going to get a ribbon today. Everyone else is going to talk themselves out of it."

Train yourself to have a positive mental attitude. If you think you can, you can. If you think you can't, you're right. Train yourself to like rough conditions. Train yourself to like hard cross-country courses. This is where the true value of the sport lies, when you surmount fears and difficulties to achieve success.

Make sure that you are on time for the briefing and course walk, as any additions, deletions, or changes to the speed and endurance test will be announced at this time. When you are going around the Roads and Tracks phase, A and C, make sure to stand and look down the track so that you see the same route that you will see while you are trotting on your horse. It does not make any sense to ride around Phase A and Phase C sitting down in the back of a pickup truck, looking where you have been. Look where you are going.

If possible, you would like to walk A and C only once, as this a great savings in your time and energy. Phase B should be walked twice, the first time during the official course walking in order to find the start and finish flags, any mandatory markers, and to look at the fences as you go around. Your second walk should be devoted to measuring the course, making sure that it is the published length, and that you know the quarter, half, and three-quarter markers. Walk Phase B on the line that you intend to ride. Avoid walking in large groups, giggling about the last competitors' party. Instead, walk with either a more experienced rider or your coach. Listen to what he has to say, and try to apply it to your horse.

Know the routes to and from the start, how the finish of Phase C relates to the vet box, where the finish for D is, and where the cooling-out area is. In addition you want to know where the warm-up areas for dressage and show jumping are, where the access is to the main arenas, and where you can hack out.

I failed to do this in Mexico in the 1968 Olympics, and when they called my number I suddenly found that, not knowing how to get into the arena, Kilkenny and I had to jump a small ditch in order to get across to the path. This did nothing to calm his already unsettled dressage attitude or my nerves. Possibly, by knowing my way to the arena, I could have saved a few points. But then again, knowing Kilkenny, maybe not. He is the only horse I ever rode that had his "game face" on every day of his life.

Whether your dressage ride is on Thursday or Friday, make sure that you are on time. Nothing is more disconcerting than to have to hurry in your preparation and warm-up. If you have any extra time, use that to visualize your ride. Plan your transitions, and rehearse in your mind the way that you are going to ride the good and bad parts of the test as your particular horse deals with it. If you have a great deal of extra time, read the rule book's definitions of paces, movements, transitions, and so on, in order to have a clear picture in your mind of exactly what it is the judges will be looking for. Try to ride your horse throughout the week, but especially during the final preparation and the actual test, as if you were in a good mood, and not mad at your horse or ashamed of your performance.

If you do compete on Thursday, your horse should have a short gallop on Friday morning. Trot for five minutes three times, all with two-minute intervals, and then give him one five-minute gallop set, starting at 400 and increasing to the cross-country speed of your level, holding that for the last minute. In the final preparatory gallops, your horse will have lost weight, especially around the withers. Consequently, he may need some extra padding in order to keep the saddle from rubbing him and giving him a withers sore.

This is not a required gallop at all. Just make sure that, whatever you do, you do not take any energy from the horse. Hand-walk the horse that afternoon. He should continue on his normal grain rations and normal hay through Friday night. If your horse goes before noon on Saturday, do not give him any hay Saturday morning. If he goes after noon, he can have a flake early Saturday morning and a short hand walk in order to keep him occupied. Saturday morning the horse should be fed and watered according to his start time.

If you are riding at the Intermediate level or higher, you should have already checked your weight pad and made sure that your weight will be, at least, 165 pounds when you start Phase A. If it is hot, you should be a few pounds over, as you may lose weight through sweating.

Phases A and C should be viewed as an exercise in horsemanship as much as warm-up and cool-down phases. There will be places where you scramble up steeper inclines, when you should allow your horse to walk. There will be stretches with level footing and a slight downhill slope where a quiet, seated, show jump canter on a loose rein may be the most efficient way to go across the ground. Use all three paces on the Roads and Tracks as the horse uses different sets of muscles and, thus, does not wear himself out at any one pace.

On Phase A look for a place where you can have a 100- to 200-meter canter just before the end. Your normal horse's paces will cause you to arrive about two minutes early. Use this time after going through the finish line to check your girth, put away any loose straps that may have shaken loose, check your galloping boots, and review the quarter, half, and three-quarter times in your mind once more.

Do not attempt to enter the start box too soon. Wait at the front of the box by walking in a small circle until the timer says, "fifteen seconds." Then walk in and let your horse rest his chest against the back of the start box. Keep him on a short, loose rein. If he moves sideways, allow him to walk in a small circle inside the start box. If you are facing away from the timer, and he says, "five seconds," you can allow your horse to start to walk and turn toward the start line. As the timer says "Go," remember to start your watch. At that moment you are already late, as the watch is already averaging steeplechase speed, while you are still standing in the start box. Get going!

Soften the reins, let the horse come out of the box in a relaxed frame with a slightly low head and neck carriage, and get going now. If the horse tends to run off, you do not want to come out of the start box pulling backward, as you then will have to support him for the entire two miles. During the steeplechase phase be sure that you ride extremely tight lines whenever possible on the turns. Concentrate on getting the horse to jump out of his stride, not to lengthen his stride. Every time you ask the horse to stand off, you take more energy out of the horse's tank than you need to in order to get over a small brush fence. Think of Phase B as a place to save your horse, not to use him up.

On the completion of Phase B take your time cantering down and pulling up. Phase C is the only start line that you get a running start at and you would like to take advantage of it. If you gallop through the finish line of B, you have, in effect, galloped onto the Roads and Tracks of Phase C. This means that, if you then pull up to a canter, then a slow canter, then a trot, then a walk, that you are actually ahead of the average for the first minute or so.

Your horse should walk anywhere from one to five minutes, depending on his type, the weather, and the distance of Phase C (a shorter Phase C gives you less time to make up minutes per kilometer and also gives your horse less time to recover). Again, as on Phase A, Phase C should be looked at as an exercise in saving your horse. Do not just mechanically tick off kilometer markers per minute, but vary his paces according to the terrain. You will probably be instructed to trot the last 100 meters or so at the end of Phase C. This gives the veterinary panel a chance to examine your horse without taking away from your cooling-out time.

As soon as you cross the finish line of Phase C, hop down and assist the vets in getting their initial temperature, pulse, and respiration readings. Immediately take the horse to a quiet corner of the ten-minute box. Leave your saddle on with the girth loosened. It is very difficult to get your equipment back on, in a short period of time, to your satisfaction. You are much better off to loosen it and leave it. This is especially true if you are carrying a weight pad.

During the ten-minute rest phase, all of your efforts should be aimed at cooling the horse's system down. The horse has a very large mass-to-surface ratio, which gives him difficulty in dissipating the heat caused by muscular exertion. Don't be afraid of ice water. Even if the temperature feels good to you, your horse is going to be in a slightly warm condition and will welcome the application of cold water.

Do not put a wool cooler or, even worse, a rain sheet over your horse. He is not going to take a chill in the five to seven minutes that he is led around in the vet box. If you put your hand about two or three inches above his loins, you will feel the warmth radiating off his body. You must allow this to occur if you want to lower his temperature, pulse, and respiration. You don't want to seal in that heat.

You should be well enough organized to allow your groom or helpers to cool the horse down while you get all of the information that you can about the course. Remember that three-day eventing is a risk sport. Some people are going to be nervous and scared. You must learn to separate the wheat from the chaff. A quiet comment from a former Olympic rider that "the footing is a bit slippery on the turn before fence five" is invaluable information. On the other hand, a pop-eyed parent screaming that "there's a hole in the water jump" is to be taken with a grain of salt. If there were a hole in the water jump, all the water would run out. Listen to people who know what they are doing, stick to your plan, and things will turn out well.

After you have been in the vet box from five to six minutes, the veterinarians will take your horse's temperature, pulse, and respiration again. At that time you should start to reassemble your gear, set the saddle forward, tighten the girths and over-girths, check the breastplate and martingale, if any, and any boots or bandages. Do not slather Vaseline all over your horse's legs. If he is that bad a jumper, sell him, because all the grease in the world isn't going to help him slide over a tree trunk cemented in the ground. Ask the veterinarian how your horse is doing and also how your horse is doing in relation to other horses that may have already come through the vet box. While all this is going on you must keep an eye on the remaining time. You would like to get up on the horse about two minutes before your start time. This will allow you to check your girth one more time, tighten your over-girth, reset the knot in your reins, do up your helmet chinstrap, and generally get ready.

Present yourself at the start at least a minute ahead of time. Don't concentrate on the sick, nervous, oily feeling that you have in your stomach or on the alarming manner in which your knees are chattering against the saddle. Reset your watch so that you can start it when the timer says "Go"; review your quarter, half, and three-quarter times in your mind; and plan on coming out of the start box in an aggressive frame of mind, even if later on during the course you plan to ease off on your speed slightly in order to ensure that you complete the speed and endurance test.

Do not go out onto the course thinking, "I'll see how he is going before I decide how to jump the combination." You should have already gotten the information that you need in the vet box, and have made your final decisions as to what lines you will ride. You have already done the work necessary to get around the three-day event course successfully. Confidence comes from planning and preparation, and the entire emphasis throughout your training program has been on preparation, planning, and practice for the questions you will be asked on the cross-country course.

Certainly your strategy will vary according to your and your horse's experience. If it is your first time in a three-day event, your goal should be to complete all three days successfully. Be willing to take some time faults, plan on jumping some of the slower routes through the more difficult combinations, and in general learn what a three-day event is all about. As your experience increases you must place a great deal of emphasis on making the optimum time across country. Your progress through the upper levels of three-day eventing is going to be determined by your ability to produce fast and bold cross-country riding.

After completing Phase D and weighing in, whether or not everything went well, you will be required to go into a cooling-off area. Again, the faster you can get your horse to cool down, the sooner he will recover from his exertions. Make sure that you have the veterinarian panel's permission to return the horse to the stables. My father used to say that "a good horse, well prepared, will jig home from a three-day event." I have had it happen to me at the Olympics and World Championships. I can assure you that there's no better feeling than to have produced your horse in such good condition that he was able to handle the demands of the course that easily.

When you return the horse to his stall you should tend to any minor cuts or scrapes, put the horse up in stable bandages, and leave him alone in his stall with clothing suitable for the temperature and weather. In the past I routinely used to poultice my horses' legs, but in recent years I have used poultice only when the horse struck a fence. I have not found that a general use of poultice makes the horse come out any better for the final vet inspection. Late in the day you should get your horse out of his stall and hand-walk him.

After a few minutes' walk, jog the horse for a few steps and make sure he is sound.

After you have checked your horse, put him up for the night, give him as much hay as you think he will eat, and his regular grain ration. If your horse has shown any signs of stiffness, you should come back late in the evening and hand-walk him for half an hour in order to keep him from stiffening up.

The Ground Jury is going to be extremely aware of horses' soundness on Sunday. This is as it should be, and you must take every effort to produce your horse in a thoroughly and completely sound condition. Medication rules vary according to the organizing body. For example, a few medications are allowed under current AHSA rules, while no medication is allowed under current FEI rules. Try not to fall afoul of the authorities. Don't be afraid to ask the treating veterinarian from the organizing committee for advice. In addition you can use electro-magnetic blankets and cold laser as therapeutic remedies. Again, check with the official veterinarians about regulations concerning alternative therapies.

Early Sunday morning, your horse should go out for a half-hour hand walk, then be brought back in to be braided and groomed, and then be taken out again. Lead the horse from the stables at least half an hour before you think he will be presented to the Ground Jury in order to make sure that he is thoroughly warmed up.

Take the attitude that, if your horse has gone well around the speed and endurance phase, you are already a winner. Do not let the pressure of the show jumping phase get to you. It is impossible to do any better than your best, and you are going to try your best under every circumstance. Concentrate on riding well and you will find that most of the jumps stay up.

If you concentrate solely on winning, you are always going to think of yourself as a loser, because riders do not win very many three-day events. Bert de Némethy used to say that "a good feeling after the round is better than any ribbon." If you and your horse have handled the cross-country course easily, done the same level of dressage test that you have been performing during your preparatory horse trials, and are able to come back, pass the vet inspection, and jump a clean round on Sunday, then, regardless of your final placing, you have been successful.

RIDING IN THE OLYMPICS

*M*OST riders dream of riding for their country in the Olympics. Even if you never make it, this is a worthy goal and one we should talk about.

The Olympics are unique. Each one takes place over strange ground and, especially since the growing importance of television, at a time of the year when the weather can be an adverse factor. This "one-off" quality of the Olympics should be viewed as an advantage. Because they occur at an unusual time of the year, the Olympics put a premium on horsemanship as well as technical riding skills. I always felt that I had a little more of an edge when I went to a competition where no one had ever jumped any of the fences before, because I usually had a pretty good idea of my and my horse's capabilities. Many riders are uncomfortable when they are taken away from their normal routine and forced to produce their horse and themselves ready for the supreme test of horse and rider without the advantage of known conditions. So the unusual nature of the Olympics can work to your detriment, or it can work to your advantage, depending upon how you view it.

The first step to riding in the Olympics is surviving the selection process. I have tried out for the Olympics under many different systems, some of them good, some of them bad. Winning all the selection trials has a wonderful way of keeping politics out of the process. When you put up an average performance it is easy to get cut at the last minute. If you are obviously having a good year, then it is very difficult for even a hostile panel to keep you off the team. So your planning should be toward getting your horse to go his best at the right time and not worrying about beating other people out of a spot. If you win every trial, and your horse is still sound, you're going to have a spot on the team.

Study the requirements of the selection process. Make sure that you know how to get on the team. If there is an unfortunate emphasis on horse trials rather than three-day event results, you had better avail yourself of the services of a good dressage professional, because dressage is going to exert an undue influence on the process. If your performance is solely weighed in three-day events, then you should rub your hands if this plays into your strengths rather than your weaknesses.

Once you have been selected for the team it is difficult not to get caught up in the circus atmosphere surrounding the Olympics. Remember, you and your horse can always get a little better, so the emphasis should be on how you are riding, not on what time your next interview is or how you look in a photo opportunity. If you are accustomed to riding your horse at a certain time, do not allow the press to intrude on that. If they are interested in you, they will work around your schedule. And if not, it doesn't matter. If your horse goes badly, you are going to lose and the press is not going to pay you any further attention. If your horse goes well, you are going to be successful and everybody will want to know your name. Just remember to be nice to all those people on the way up . . . you are going to see them all again on the way back down.

The preparation for the Olympic Games usually includes a training session, away from home, of thirty-five to forty days. These can be disconcerting for people who have never been through them before. You will be away from familiar grounds for a long period of time, riding with people, many times, who are not well known to you. You will not have the number of horses to ride that you usually do at home and, therefore, you will have to deal with spare time.

Try to look on the training session as a wonderful experience as well as a time for you to increase your and your horse's fitness. If you are in a foreign country, take advantage of the fact that there will be other horses and riders around the area. Go and watch them, and try to learn something new. You don't have to apply it to your horse— in fact, I advise you not to—but you can certainly make some notes and go back and try some of the techniques the next winter.

Some of the extra time that you will have you should use in getting yourself fit. The extra distance that you are required to go in the Olympics will certainly have its effect on you as well as your horse.

Try to watch the other riders during their workouts. Make sure that you are always a positive and supporting teammate. Now is not the time to dwell on the negatives. Now is the time to dwell on the things you all do well and make sure that you do them well in competition.

There is a tendency, as the training session progresses, to lose your competitive nerves and magnify the task ahead. Remember that you got here by doing well in three-day events. You are getting ready to go into another three-day event. Yes, it is true that they have "moved the goalposts" and you will go a longer distance than usual. All this means is that you might go at a slightly steadier pace across country and jump one or two smaller option fences in order to save your horse. But, basically, your horse has all of the skills and talent to compete at the Olympics if you have been selected for the training session. Concentrate on doing your best in each phase.

The one thing that you must make sure of is that your horse is extra fit. This means doing gallops that will be much longer and harder than you are used to employing. Riders are, understandably, reluctant to use these works, but I assure you that you cannot be successful in the Olympics if you do not do the extra work that the increased distance demands. This extra level of fitness is going to have its effect on your horse and you must take that into account in your preparation. He will need longer to recover from each of the gallops, and he will start to show a change in his other phases, his dressage and his show jumping.

Sometimes this is for the better. Kilkenny used to sober up as we got closer to a major international competition because I could finally give him enough work to settle him down. Carawich, on the other hand, became more and more difficult as he got fitter because he knew so well how close he was to being allowed to go cross-country. Analyze your horse and deal with the problems. This is the horsemanship element that I referred to earlier. Don't let the change in your horse cause you to panic. Whatever the situation during the preparation, try to be positive. You are already capable of competing at this level. All you have to do is to continue to ride well. Other people will take care of riding badly, as they succumb to nerves and pressure. For you, pressure is what turns coal into diamonds.

Once you get to the Olympic site, everything will be completely new to everyone. There will be a great deal of wasted time, finding out where various facilities are. The best thing you can do is look at a map of the stable area and training facility. Find out not only where you can go with your horse, but also how you get back and forth from the stables to the training areas, where the security check points are, what you need to get through those security check points, and so on.

*D*AVID and Wilbur having a celebration. There is no feeling like jumping a clean, fast round over a difficult course. It makes all of the hard work, discipline, and disappointment along the way worthwhile. David O'Connor on Wilton Fair, Badminton, 1992. BRANT GAMMA

Expect things to go wrong, not so much in the training schedule, but in the fact that buses do not run at the correct times or on the correct routes, for example. This can be a bit disconcerting if you have planned to ride your horse at a certain time. Try to go out to the stables early, planning on staying there for the day unless you have private transport that you can count on. Otherwise, bring a book or a magazine and be prepared to be patient.

Whenever you are going to ride your horse, you want to get yourself settled in and mentally prepared. With any luck your horse is going to be brimming with energy and is going to present challenges to your technical riding skills. You want to be in a calm and relaxed frame of mind and ready for this, rather than have a hair-raising ride across town and jump into the saddle at the last minute, feeling flustered and irritable. It's better to be sitting on your tack trunk waiting to get on than sitting stuck in traffic.

At the Olympics in 1956 a Frenchman, Guy Lefrant, decided to pick up his mother at Stockholm airport on the day of his dressage. Returning from the airport with his mother, he got stuck in traffic and missed his dressage time, eliminating both himself and his team. (It's no surprise that he was placed under house arrest and shipped out to Algeria two days later.) I suppose the moral of this story is that Mom is on her own while you're riding in the Olympics.

Whatever the outcome, try to enjoy your stay there. You'll always remember these three days and you want to view them as the culmination of your sporting life, regardless of the outcome.

I prefer riding in the Olympics to the World Championships because of the unique nature of the Olympics. You are doing something that no one has ever done before, nor will again, whereas in the World Championships often you are competing on familiar ground. Riding in the Olympics is the greatest thrill any rider can ever have. I hope this book helps you find your way.

*T*HERE is no feeling worse than devoting a year of your life in preparation for a big event, only to have it go wrong. I'm standing alone in the cooling-out area at the World Championships, 1978, wondering what I could have done to prevent a fall at the infamous Serpent. The highs in this sport are high, but the lows are pretty low. The author at the World Championships, Lexington, 1978. CLARKSON LINDLEY

ON the other hand, winning a medal for your country in a foreign land is the pinnacle of your career. Winning it on the horse that meant more to you than any other is icing on the cake. The author winning the individual silver medal, Alternate Olympics, Fontainebleau, France, 1980, with Carawich, the "past, pluperfect, master of the game." HUGO M. CZERNY PHOTOGRAPH

APPENDIX I

Interval Notation and Conditioning Gallops

INTERVAL NOTATION

BEFORE we start talking about fitness works I want to explain some terms that I will use to describe various amounts of exercise. You will definitely need to understand this shorthand before you study the conditioning tables that follow. A normal conditioning work could be written down in the following manner: "Trot for five minutes, then give the horse a two-minute break at the walk on loose reins. Follow this by two more repetitions of the same amount of work. After trotting three repetitions of five minutes each, all with two-minute walk intervals, canter a four-minute set, take a two-minute walk interval, then repeat the four-minute canter set for two more repetitions. The horse will trot for a total of fifteen minutes and canter for a total of twelve minutes. The horse will exercise for a total of thirty-seven minutes from start to finish." Based on my interval notation the work described above would look like this:

$$5'' \ 220 \times 3w \ / \ 2'' \ i$$

$$+$$

$$4'' \ 400 \times 3w \ / \ 2'' \ i.$$

Interval notation that looks like this, 5″ 220 × 3w / 2″ i + 6″ 400 × 3w / 2″ i, is read "trot at 220 meters per minute for five minutes (5″220). Repeat three times (×3) with two-minute intervals of walk between each set (w/2″i). Then (+) canter six minutes (6″400) three times (×3) with two-minute intervals of walk between each set (w/2″i)." Or, fifteen minutes of trot and eighteen minutes of canter.

Interval notation is a flexible system and can be used to describe quite complex gallops. For example, an Advanced horse might do a gallop that looks like this:

$$5″\ 220 \times 3\text{w} / 2″\ \text{i} +$$
$$8″\ 400 \rightarrow 520\ (2)\ \text{w}/\ 2″\ \text{i} +$$
$$6″\ 500 \rightarrow 650\ (1)$$

This is read as "trot five minutes three times with two-minute intervals. Then canter for eight minutes, starting at 400 meters per minute, and increasing speed gradually, finally reaching 520 meters per minute and holding that speed for the last two minutes of the set. After a two-minute walk interval, canter again for six minutes, starting at 500 meters per minute and increasing to 650 meters per minute, holding that speed for the last minute."

This same work can be further analyzed by breaking the above gallops down using the following tables: 8″400 → 520(2) should be performed in this sequence:

2″ @ 400 =	800	meters
2″ @ 450 =	900	meters
2″ @ 500 =	1,000	meters
2″ @ 520 =	1,040	meters
8″	3,740	meters

This set is followed in two minutes by:

2″ @ 500 =	1,000	meters
2″ @ 550 =	1,100	meters
1″ @ 600 =	600	meters
1″ @ 650 =	650	meters
6″	3,350	meters

SPEED

*O*BVIOUSLY, this gallop is not for every horse. A horse that can safely and adequately perform this work is probably two to three weeks away from a 3-Star CCI or a month away from a 4-Star CCI, the Olympics, or the World Championships. This system puts a premium on your knowing the speed you are going at all times on any horse.

Some riders have trouble with this, and the easiest way to deal with it is to find an area with good footing and use a meter wheel or measuring tape to define certain distances. You should know the basic conditioning speed, 400 meters per minute. You should then know 500 meters a minute and the cross-country speed of your level, whether 520, 550, or 570 meters per minute. The best way to find 570 meters a minute is to measure off this distance on the ground, put markers at the start and finish, and then canter through this distance until you absorb the rhythm of the horse's stride at this speed. The same should be done for 600 meters per minute and for the steeplechase speed of your level. Make sure the footing is good before practicing these speeds.

CONDITIONING GALLOPS

I HAVE designed this list of gallops to make them progressive in their difficulty. You should be able to take a horse that has been in light work for sixty days and start this program. However, you do *not* have to do all of these gallops to get your horse fit. As the work gets more complex, you have to consider the effects of your terrain, weather, frequency of competition in horse trials, and most important, footing. Trot your horse for 5″ three times, with 2″ intervals, as a warm-up, before each canter exercise, or in my notation, 5″ 220 × 3 w/ 2″ i.

1. 3″ 350 × 3 w/ 2″ i (repeat twice with three days between canters).

2. 4″ 400 × 3 w/ 2″ i (repeat three times with three days between canters).

3. 6″ 400 × 3 w/ 2″ i (repeat three times with four days between gallops).

This eight-gallop sequence should take you thirty days to complete. By this stage a Thoroughbred horse should be fit to go around his first Preliminary horse trials of the season, without trying to make the time.

4. 8″ 400 × 3 w/ 2″ i. I usually use this work for Intermediate and above.

5. 6″ 400 w/ 2″ i +
   6″ 400 → 450 w/ 2″ i +
   6″ 400 → 500

6. 6″ 400 w/ 2″ i +
   5″ 450 w/ 2″ i +
   4″ 500

7. 6″ 400 → 450 w/ 2″ i +
   6″ 400 → 450 (1″)
   → 520 (1″)

8. 6″ 400 → 520 (1″) w 2″ i +
   6″ 400 → 600 (1″)

9. 6″ 400 → 520 (2″) w/ 2″ i +
   6″ 500 → 650 (1″)

10. 6″ 400 → 520 (2″) w/ 2″ i +
    6″ 500 → 650 (2″)

Any Thoroughbred horse that has done all of the slow conditioning canters (3–4's, 3–6's, etc.) and at least half of the speed intervals, should be fit for a Preliminary three-day event. I use the following gallops for Intermediate three-day event horses:

11. 8″ 400 → 550 (1″) w/ 2″ i +
    6″ 500 → 650 (1″)

12. 8″ 400 → 550 (2″) w/ 2″ i +
    6″ 500 → 650 (2″)

Horses aiming for an Intermediate three-day event should be fit after completing these workouts. The following workouts are usually for Advanced horses:

13. 8″ 400 → 570 (1″) w/ 2″ i +
    5″ 500 → 700 (1″)

14. 8″ 400 → 570 (2″) w/ 2″ i +
    4″ 500 → 700 (2″)

15. 6″ 400 → 450 (1″) w/ 2″ i +
    9″ 450 → 500
          → 550
          → 600

16. 6″ 400 → 500 w/ 2″ i +
    10″ 500 → 550
           → 600
           → 650

17. 8″ 400 → 600 (1″) w/ 2″ i +
    6″ 500 → 700 (1″)

18. 6″ 400 → 600 (2″) w/ 2″ i +
    4″ 500 → 800

19. 6″ 400 → 600 (2″) w/ 2″ i +
    4″ 600 → 1000

These four last workouts are designed for CCI*** and CCI**** levels. Unless your footing is perfect, they should take place on a sand track. Again, not all these workouts need to be done to get the horse fit. If possible, hill work should be substituted for speed work. It is difficult to quantify hill work in any meaningful form, so you must learn each hill's workload as you use it.

APPENDIX II

Sample Schedules

*T*HERE are four sample schedules in this appendix. These schedules cover the range of FEI three-day events, from CCI* to CCI****. I have chosen four very different horses for illustration, as I want you to see how flexible scheduling must be to produce fit horses. Of the four horses, three of them won their event, and the fourth, Carawich, was fifth at Badminton.

One Star

Bright Idea was a fourteen-year-old, 15.3 hand, brown Irish 7/8 Thoroughbred gelding. He had a very calm temperament, and the normal wear and tear of a horse his age. Note that he was led out a great deal, instead of being ridden. I did not feel any great pressure to train him every day, thus, the occasional day off.

Two Stars

Killarney was a ten-year-old, 17 hand, chestnut Thoroughbred gelding. He was the only horse to make the optimum time at Radnor that year, and made it look easy. He had white feet and this caused us a lot of trouble with his shoeing. Killarney convinced me not to "drill" horses in the final preparation, but rather to "taper" them. Note the presence of an easy week in Killarney's final preparation. Killarney went from calm to nervous, and back again, very quickly. Thus, we would walk him some days and longe and jog him in the fields on others, according to his mood.

Three Stars

Alex was an eleven-year-old, 17 hand, brown Thoroughbred gelding. He was probably the laziest Thoroughbred I have ever dealt with. He was by Crème de la Crème, but he hid his class under a bushel. I loved him anyway, and used a lot of turn-out and leading to keep him fresh. I never drilled him, but I did use more speed than usual, many times in company with other horses.

Four Stars

Carawich was an eleven-year-old, 16.3 hand, brown Irish 7/8 Thoroughbred gelding. Because Badminton is so difficult, one tends to prepare horses as if they were going to the Olympics. The interval works in Carawich's schedule are about as long and hard as you would ever ask a horse to go. The weather in England was vile that year, and we missed an important event due to snow. Thus, the unusual intensity of the gallops, which took place on ideal footing.

In the schedules that follow, SJ = show jump, and m/m = meters per minute.

BRIGHT IDEA, ESSEX 1992, CCI*

Day 45. 5″ 220 × 3w / 2″ i +
6″ 400 × 3w / 2″ i

44. 1½-hr. led out

43. 1-hr. + dressage

42. 1-hr. + SJ curved lines and related distances 3′3″

41. 1 hr. + dressage

40. 5″ 220 × 3w / 2″ i +
6″ 400 × 3w / 2″ i

39. 2-hr. walk—led out

38. 1 hr. + dressage

37. 1 hr. + SJ gymnastics 3′3″

36. 1 hr. + dressage

35. 5″ 220 × 3w / 2″ i +
6″ 400 × 3w / 2″ i

34. 2-hr. walk—led out

33. 1 hr. + dressage

32. 1 hr. + SJ 3'6" fences

31. 1 hr. + dressage

30. 5" 220 × 3w / 2" i +
    8" 400 × 3w / 2" i

29. 2-hr. walk—led out

28. 1 hr. + dressage

27. 1 hr. + SJ 3'6" fences

26. Field dressage 45"

25. 5" 220 × 3w / 2" i +
    8" 400 × 3w / 3" i

24. 2-hr. walk—led out

23. 1 hr. + dressage

22. 1 hr. + SJ individual fences 3'6"

21. 1½-hr. walk

20. 5" 220 × 3w / 2" i +
    8" 400 × 3w / 2" i

19. Turn out ½ day

18. 1 hr. + dressage

17. SJ individual fences 3'6" + canter 2 long hills

16. 1 hr. + dressage

15. 5" 220 × 3w / 2" i +
    8" 400 → 520 (2") +
    6" 500 → 650 (1")

14. Turn out ½ day

13. 1 hr. + dressage

12. Individual SJ fences 3'6" + canter 2 long hills

11. 1 hr. + dressage

10. 5" 220 × 3w / 2" i +
    8" 400 → 550 (2") +
    4" 500 → 700 (1")

9. Turn out ½ day

8. 1-hr. walk + dressage

7. SJ course 3′6″ + canter 2 long hills

6. Fair Hill Horse Trials Dressage and Show Jumping

5. Fair Hill Horse Trials X-C Test

4. Ship to event

3. 1-hr. walk—led out

2. Field dressage 45″

1. Ride-in
Essex CCI*—Dressage
—Speed and Endurance
—Show Jumping

KILLARNEY, RADNOR 1982, CCI**

Day 45. 1½-hr. walk

44. X-C school—pulled shoe

43. Hand-walked

42. Replaced shoe, 30″ longe A.M.—ship to horse trials

41. Mar Hill Horse Trials—Dressage and Show Jumping

40. Mar Hill Horse Trials—Cross-Country

39. Turn out

38. 1¾-hr. walk

37. 1-hr. walk + 30″ dressage

36. 1-hr. walk + 30″ dressage

35. Dressage clinic

34. 5″ 220 × 3w / 2″ i +
6″ 400 × 1w / 2″ i +
8″ 400 × 2w / 2″ i

33. $1^3/_4$-hr. walk

32. 1-hr. walk + SJ individual fences 3'6"–3'9"

31. 1-hr. walk, including 5" 220 × 3w / 2" i +
    45" dressage

30. 5" 220 × 3w / 2" i +
    8" 400 × 3w / 2" i

29. $1^3/_4$-hr. walk

28. 1-hr. walk, including 5" 220 × 3w / 2" i +
    45" dressage

27. SJ individual fences 3'9"

26. Dressage clinic

25. 5" 220 × 3w / 2" i +
    6" 400 → 450 (1") w / 2" i +
    8" 450 → 520 (2")

24. 2-hr. walk

23. 1-hr. walk on hills + 45" dressage

22. $1^1/_2$-hr. hack, including 5" 220 × 2w / 2" i +
    10" 220 × 2w / 2" i

21. $1^1/_2$-hr. walk on hills

20. 5" 220 × 3w / 2" i +
    6" 400 → 450 (2") w / 2" i +
    8" 450 → 550 (2")

19. $1^3/_4$-hr. hack including 5" 220 × 2w / 2" i

18. Longe 30" + SJ individual fences 3'9"

17. 1-hr. walk on hills + 45" dressage

16. 1-hr. walk + 5" 220 × 2w / 2" i +
    4" 400 × 1w / 2" i +
    3 × hill, 1 @ 400, 1 @ 450, 1 @ 500

15. 1-hr. walk + 5" 220 × 3w / 2" i

14. Longed 30" + 45" dressage

13. Lame—close nails in both front legs

12. Hand-walked and poulticed

11. Hand-walked and poulticed

10. Hand-walked and poulticed

9. Hand-walked and poulticed

8. 1½-hr. walk

7. 1-hr. walk + 30″ dressage

6. SJ 3′9″ individual fences +
   slow canter up 2 steep hills

5. 1½-hr. walk plus 30″ dressage

4. Slow canter up 3 long hills

3. 2-hr. walk

2. Ship to Radnor. 1-hr. walk + 1-hr. field dressage

1. 1-hr. walk + 1-hr. ride-in

   Radnor CCI**—Dressage
   —Speed and Endurance
   —Show Jumping

ALEX, CHESTERLAND 1980, CCI***

Day 45. 30″ dressage + 1 hr. hack

44. 5″ 220 × 3w / 2″ i +
   6″ 400 × 3w / 2″ i

43. 1-hr. lead

42. 30″ dressage + 1-hr. hack

41. SJ 3′6″ individual fences + 1-hr. hack

40. 30″ dressage + 1-hr. hack

39. 5″ 220 × 3w / 2″ i +
   6″ 400 × 3w / 2″ i

38. 1-hr. lead

37. 30″ dressage + 1-hr. hack

36. 3′9″–4′ individual SJ fences + 1-hr. hack

35. 30″ dressage + 1-hr. hack

34. 5″ 220 × 3w / 2″ i +
    8″ 400 × 3w / 2″ i

33. Turn out

32. 30″ dressage + 1-hr. hack

31. 3′9″ lines and turns SJ + 1-hr. lead

30. 30″ dressage + 1-hr. lead

29. 5″ 220 × 3w / 2″ i +
    8″ 400 × 3w / 2″ i

28. Turn out

27. 1½-hr. lead

26. 3′9″ SJ course + 1-hr. lead

25. 30″ dressage + 1-hr. lead

24. 5″ 220 × 3w / 2″ i +
    8″ 400 → 500 (2″) +
    6″ 400 → 520

23. 1-hr. lead

22. 30″ dressage + 1-hr. lead

21. Ship and ride-in

20. Mar Hill Horse Trials Dressage and Show Jumping

19. Mar Hill Horse Trials X-C

18. Turn out

17. 1½-hr. lead

16. 1½-hr. lead

15. 1-hr. lead + SJ gymnastics

14. 30″ dressage + 1-hr. lead

13. 5″ 220 × 3w / 2″ i +
    6″ 400 → 450 +
    8″ 400 → 600

12. 1½-hr. lead

11. 30″ dressage + 1-hr. lead

10. 3′9″ SJ practice + gallop 2 hills

9. 30″ dressage + 1-hr. lead
8. 5″ 220 × 3w / 2″ i +
    6″ 400 → 600 +
    4″ 600 → 1,000
7. 1½-hr. hack
6. 30″ dressage + 1-hr. lead
5. 4′ SJ course
4. Gallop up 3 hills
3. Dressage + 1-hr. hack
2. Ship to event, 1-hr. walk
1. 30″ longe A.M., 30″ hand walk P.M.
    Chesterland, CCI*** —Dressage
    —Cross-Country
    —Show Jumping

CARAWICH, BADMINTON 1979, CCI****

Day 45. 2-hr. hack
44. 1-hr. hack + 45″ dressage
43. Ship to JFK
42. Ship to England
41. Arrive England 6 A.M., hand walk P.M.
40. 1½-hr. hack A.M. + dressage P.M. +
    10″ canter @ 350 m/m
39. 2-hr. hack A.M. + dressage show P.M.
38. 2-hr. hack A.M. + 45″ dressage
37. 2-hr. hack A.M. + gymnastic show jumps P.M.
36. 5″ 220 × 3w / 2″ i +
    14″ 400 × 2w / 2″ i +
    canter 2 hills
35. 2-hr. hack A.M. + 30″ dressage P.M.

34. X-C school 20 efforts fence by fence

33. 2-hr. hack

32. 2-hr. hack + canter 3 short steep hills A.M., 30″ dressage P.M.

31. 5″ 220 × 3w / 2″ i +
    8″ 400 +
    8″ 400 → 450 (1″) +
    8″ 400 → 500 (2″)

30. 1¼-hr. hack A.M., 1-hr. dressage P.M.

29. X-C school 15 fences 2,400 meters @ 520 m/m

28. 2-hr. walk

27. 1-hr. hack, 30″ dressage P.M.

26. 1½-hr. walk and trot on hills A.M., SJ individual fences P.M.

25. 2-hr. hack

24. 5″ 220 × 3w / 2″ i +
    8″ 400 × 3w / 2″ i

23. 2-hr. hack + 30″ dressage

22. 1-hr. hack + 45″ dressage

21. 2-hr. A.M. hack + SJ 3′9″ course

20. Dressage—Rushall Horse Trials

19. SJ 4′ course A.M., X-C Event 4,200 meters @ 555 m/m P.M.

18. Hand-walk 30″ A.M. and P.M.

17. 2-hr. hack

16. 2-hr. hack and dressage

15. 1-hr. hack and dressage

14. 20″ slow canter A.M. + 3′9″ SJ course P.M.

13. Dressage show

12. Dressage show

11. 5″ 220 × 3w / 2″ i +
    6″ 400 → 450 +
    9″ → 500

$\rightarrow$ 550
$\rightarrow$ 600

10. 2-hr. A.M. hack + 45″ dressage P.M.

9. 1½-hr. hack A.M. + 45″ dressage P.M.

8. 5″ 220 × 3w / 2″ i +
6″ 400 $\rightarrow$ 500 +
10″ 500 $\rightarrow$ 550
$\rightarrow$ 600
$\rightarrow$ 650

7. 1½-hr. hack

6. 1½-hr. hack + SJ 4′ course

5. 1-hr. hack A.M. + 1-hr. dressage P.M.

4. 5″ 220 × 3w / 2″ i +
6″ 400 $\rightarrow$ 500 +
6″ 500 $\rightarrow$ 650 +
5″ 400 $\rightarrow$ 650
$\rightarrow$ 800

3. Ship and hack

2. Ride-in

1. Ride-in

Badminton, CCI****—Dressage
—Cross-Country
—Show Jumping

Hack = walk on the buckle
Ride-in = work designed to relax your particular horse
lead = led from another horse

APPENDIX III

Gymnastic Show Jumping

ERE are a few general comments before we discuss the specific exercises in this appendix.

Set these exercises up using 12-foot rails as much as possible; if you do not have enough rails and standards, you can do many of the exercises simply by setting up one group of fences and then changing the distances and setting up another; if you are not sure about your horse, make the fence too low rather than too high.

While practicing the exercises in this appendix, keep your eyes fixed on the next object. If that is the first rail on the ground, watch the rail until it disappears between your horse's ears and then look at the last rail in the cavalletti series. If it is an obstacle, look at it until it goes out of sight between your horse's ears. This will help you maintain the exact line that you had preselected, as well as develop your timing. Timing is the art of seeing your stride. You can't see your stride if you don't look at the jump.

COURSE #1

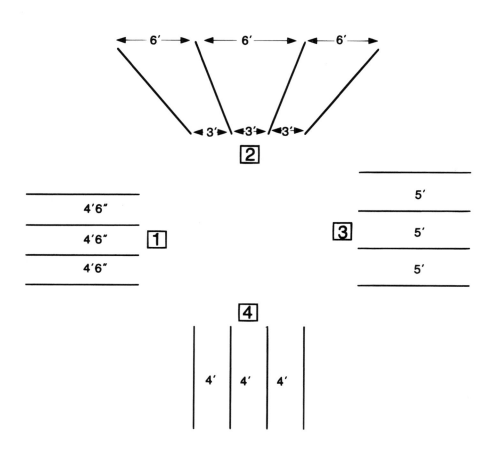

COURSE ONE

*T*HE first course can be done in a dressage saddle or a jumping saddle. Use a medium length of stirrup. The horse's back is more active over cavalletti rails and you will need more security than you do working on the flat. For all cavalletti work your horse should wear leg protection, as he may knock his legs together while learning to step over the rails.

After you have warmed your horse up at the walk, trot, and canter, trot into the exercise marked #1 in the sketch. This exercise will produce a working trot for most horses. If your horse is extremely green, pull the first and the third rails in toward the center line. This will produce a 9-foot distance between two rails. Horses find this exercise easy, and soon become stable and regular at the trot. Then put the four rails together and work in both directions over exercise #1.

After you have established your horse's balance and rhythm at #1, proceed to #2. Work on a circle through this exercise. Keep your horse adjusted so that while he is on a curve, the length of his step feels the same as in #1. Once you have become adept at this, you can enter closer to the 3-foot end of the rails, where the distance is shorter, and let the horse angle away from the center of the circle. Your horse will go from a working trot to a lengthened stride or even to a couple of steps of extended trot. Alternatively, enter from the 6-foot distance, where the horse is taking quite a large step, and angle in toward the 3-foot distance. This will bring your horse back to a working trot or even to a slightly collected trot. Having successfully gone both directions over #2, including being able to angle both ways, proceed to #3.

Exercise #3 will produce the sensation of extended trot, and you may find that your horse is incapable of handling the fourth rail. Take one rail away and continue. You will find that after a couple of days of work over cavalletti, your horse gets the message and you can add the fourth rail. Work in both directions over the 5-foot cavalletti rails until your horse can maintain his regularity and length of stride.

After a short break, proceed to exercise #4. These four rails on the ground, 4 feet apart, will produce the sensation of a collected trot. All of these exercises can be ridden posting or sitting, but you should definitely use a rising trot until you and your horse become adjusted to them. Again, practice both ways until your horse is relaxed and steady in his rhythm and balance, and able to deal with the rails without any interruption in the flow of his movement.

After another short break, link the exercises together in order to produce the various transitions and paces that will be required by your dressage test. For example, enter from the bottom left, use the working trot over exercise #1, the 4-foot, 6-inch rails, turn right in such a fashion that you produce an arc through exercise #2, which causes the horse to collect his step. In other words, enter from outside in. This will put the horse in a slightly collected frame. Proceed directly to exercise #3, which will produce an extended trot. After the extended trot, turn and enter the collected exercise at #4.

If you have successfully done this, walk, pat your horse, and let him relax and consider his effort while you plan your next series of repetitions through these exercises.

Take a moment to remind yourself of your horse's bad habits. If your horse tends to rush at the trot, he does not need too many applications of #3. He should come from outside in rather than from inside out at exercise #2. If, on the other hand, your horse is choppy-strided or lazy, a bit more emphasis on exercise #3 and a few more repetitions at #2, going from inside out, will teach him to extend his stride. The total amount of exercise over these rails should not exceed forty minutes, including the breaks.

COURSE TWO

$\mathcal{S}$TART work over Course Two with four rails set on the ground 4 feet 6 inches apart and one more rail 9 feet away on the ground at #1 so that you have five poles on the ground. Trot back and forth several times to establish your horse's rhythm and balance, then raise the rail at #1 to produce a suitable warm-up fence (usually between 18 and 24 inches). Trot only from the cavalletti rails toward the rail at #1. You can repeat this several times. You can also further raise the rail at #1. Horses that are in consistent work should be able to trot through the cavalletti and jump a rail at #1 set at the level of their division. They should be able to land calmly and in balance.

After you have warmed up over #1, put it back down to approximately 18 inches and put a rail at #2 about 2 feet high. This will produce an exercise of four cavalletti rails and two vertical fences. Again, trot in, jump the first obstacle as before, land, take one stride, and jump out. After several repetitions, you may raise the rail at #2. Keep in mind that the performance of your horse is a greater judge of how rapidly you can progress in terms of raising the fences than some preselected idea that you or I might have.

Once the horse is comfortable with the one-stride exercise, lower #2 and add an oxer at #3. Make sure that the front rail at #3 is level with, or slightly higher than, the rail at #2. Jump this oxer several times before you start to raise it. It is a good idea to finish with the obstacle at the size and spread required by your level of competition.

COURSE #2

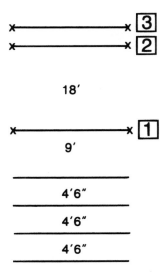

COURSE #3

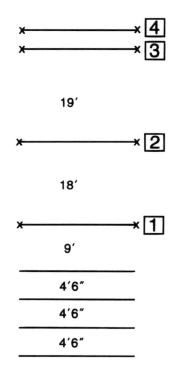

COURSE THREE

*C*OURSE Three is a continuation of the work that was done in Course Two. Start again with the rails taken away at #2, #3, and #4, leaving only their open standards and one rail on the ground at #1. Warm the horse up as before. Then repeat the same procedure for #1 and #2 until you are working through the obstacles at a comfortable height. If you have raised the obstacle at #2 to slightly above the level of your division, you should lower that fence again before adding a rail at #3. For example, a Preliminary horse should be jumping obstacles set in the following manner. The first time that you confront the entire sequence of obstacles, they should probably be 2 feet at #1, 3 feet at #2, 3 feet 3 inches at #3 and #4. This should be quite easy for a Preliminary horse with some experience. If your horse loses a bit of confidence as the jumps get higher, immediately lower the obstacles and narrow the spread until his confidence has returned.

The distance between the three obstacles will produce a one-stride from #1 to #2, and a one-stride from #2 to #3. Strive for balance and regularity here. If your horse gets too close to #2 and #3, put a pole on the ground exactly half the distance between #1 and #2, and again between #2 and #3. This will make your horse land sooner after #1 and #2, thus giving him more distance in front of #2 and #3–4 to complete his stride.

COURSE #4

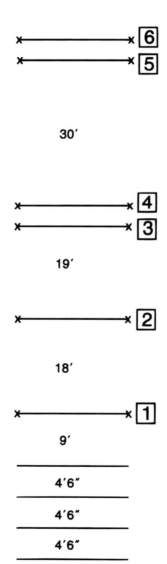

COURSE FOUR

*A*GAIN, this exercise is a continuation of the previous courses. The only difference here is that the horse will now trot in, land over obstacle #1, take one stride, jump #2, take one stride, jump #3–4, then take two strides and jump #5–6. Work systematically through this exercise as you did in the preceding ones. Do not add the next rail until you are sure the horse understands the problems posed by this rail. If you have raised one of the fences to the maximum height for your competitive level, make sure that you lower it before you add the next obstacle. When you increase the technicality of an exercise, you should decrease the height and spread until you are sure that the horse understands what you want from him.

COURSE FIVE

$\mathscr{C}$OURSE Five is a good exercise for horses that tend to quicken on course, and for riders that have trouble maintaining a balanced two-point. Start with all of the rails removed except the placing rail and the rail at #1 set at 24 inches. After jumping several times from the placing rail to the fence, work in the opposite direction. This means you will be approaching the fence through a line of open standards with one rail set at 2 feet in the standards at #1. The horse will approach at the trot, jump the small obstacle, land, and step over the 9-foot rail without attempting to put in a stride. This will teach your horse to bounce this distance. Occasionally a horse will be startled by the rail on the ground and refuse or overjump badly. If he overjumps and lands beyond the placing rail, move the rail out until the horse lands inside the placing rail. Then you can gradually move the rail back in to 9 feet. Make sure that you repeat this exercise until the horse understands it, as this is a key exercise to teaching horses to jump a bounce.

Once you're confident of your horse's attitude, place a rail 2 feet high in the standards at #2. Trot back and forth several times from the placing rail into the bounce and back from the bounce to the placing rail. After this you should add a rail at #3. Repeat once or twice each way and continue to #4, then #5, and so on. When the entire exercise has been constructed, the horse will approach at the trot, jump the first rail, bounce, bounce again, land, take one stride, bounce, bounce again, and canter out over the last 9-foot rail. Concentrate on maintaining your two-point throughout the entire exercise so that the horse's back can move freely underneath you. If you are fairly experienced in your jumping, you may relax to the horse's back during the 20-foot part of the exercise and take one stride while sitting lightly on the saddle.

If you are having trouble with the exercise, use a neck strap and make yourself stay in a two-point position. Concentrate especially on keeping a light, supple contact between your elbow and the horse's mouth. This exercise causes the head and neck of the horse to move

COURSE #5

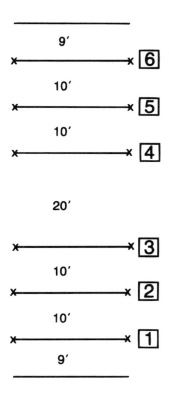

back and forth in a pronounced fashion. Learn how to keep your hand connected exactly to your horse's mouth throughout his jumping motion. The motion of your horse's head and neck when he jumps is not forward and back. The motion of the horse's head and neck when he jumps is back, forward, and back. Stay connected to the horse with the reins throughout the exercise by following this motion.

COURSE SIX

*P*ROCEED here as in Course Two. Trot your horse over exercises #1, then the oxers at #2 and #3. The obstacles at #4, #5, #6, and #7 should be built before you start work. Build the oxers at #6 and #7 with a diagonal pole across the top of each oxer. These oxers will get rather wide, and the diagonal pole keeps your horse from thinking the oxer is a bounce. After that, unless you have a knockdown, your course is set.

Next, trot back and forth over #4 and #5, with the obstacles set at 24 to 30 inches. The distance from #4 to #5 is a slightly short stride. As your horse's front feet touch the ground, land in a light three-point, squeeze the reins, and use your voice to slow him down. Wait for the horse to take a full stride before jumping again. The sensation should be that of slow motion rather than increasing rapidity as your horse jumps #4 and #5. Repeat several times in both directions until you are quite sure that your horse can handle trotting over 3-foot rails, 16 feet apart, producing one short stride.

Then proceed to the oxers at #6 and #7. These should be 2 feet high but 3 feet wide and 32 feet apart. (Later on, these oxers can be 2 feet high and up to 6 feet wide, still with diagonal rails on top.) This will produce quite a long two-stride exercise. Approach at a strong trot with the reins very soft. The oxers are set purposefully low. Do not worry about knocking one down but, rather, worry about getting across the distance. As the horse leaves the ground at #6, close your heels and think to yourself that you are riding across a ditch rather than jumping an oxer. As you land, your action is the reverse of landing after #4. This time you must close your heels, cluck to your horse, make sure the reins are soft, take two long strides, and jump again.

Thirty-two feet is quite long from the trot, and I find that many horses will tend to chip in a third stride at first. Support your leg with your stick at the point of takeoff in front of the first oxer if necessary. Repeat this exercise several times from #6 to #7 until your horse starts to anticipate leaving long in two strides. Then

COURSE #6

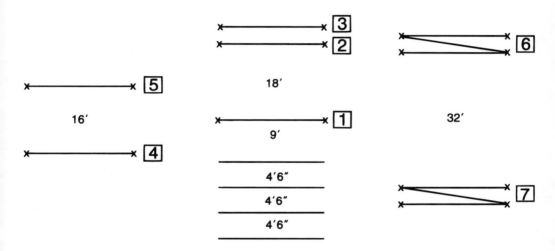

come back the other direction, from #7 to #6, one or two more times, and then walk and give your horse a break.

Now you should start to design mini-courses that will help you deal with your horse's particular problems. For example, if you have a horse that rushes, you should emphasize turning from #1, #2–3 back to #4–5 rather than continuing to drill your horse through the long distance of #6–7. The horse that handles the long distance should practice it occasionally but not continually. If your horse is sticky, you should emphasize #1, #2–3, and #6–7. Riders have a tendency to deal with exercises that they feel comfortable with. Instead, you should emphasize the exercise your horse finds more difficult. Practice jumping on a steady stride, a short stride, or a long stride until you feel comfortable with any variation in your horse's stride.

COURSE SEVEN

$\mathscr{C}$OURSE Six taught you and your horse to shorten and lengthen your stride between obstacles. Course Seven now asks that you lengthen and shorten your horse's stride between obstacles in close proximity to each other.

Take away the rails at #2, #3, and #4 so that you produce your usual warm-up fence. After the horse has warmed up over #1, raise this rail in 6-inch increments until you reach the height of your competitive level. Once your horse has jumped this to your satisfaction, walk, set the rail at #1 at 2 feet, and repeat this exercise at #2, starting at 3 feet and raising it to 3 feet 6 inches. After several repetitions, give your horse a break. Replace the rail at #2 to 3 feet and build a low, wide oxer at #3. The oxer should be 2 feet in height but a minimum of 3 feet 6 inches in spread, with a diagonal rail across the top of the oxer. Now trot through the cavalletti, jump the obstacle at #1, land, take a normal stride, and jump #2. (This part of the exercise is similar to the exercise that you did between obstacles #6 and #7 in Course Six.)

As you land over #2, soften the reins, close your legs, and ride the horse forward in his stride. You should take only one stride in that 20-foot distance. Practice #1, #2, and #3 several times, making the spread of the oxer 6 inches greater each time. You should be able to jump a 2-foot oxer with a 6-foot spread quite easily.

Then walk, return the spread of the oxer to 4 feet, and add a rail 3 feet high in the standards at #4. Make sure that the distance is 19 feet from the back of the oxer as it presently exists and not as it existed when you originally constructed the course. Different horses may jump a different spread, which changes the distance from the oxer to the last vertical. You are now in a situation where you will trot in over the cavalletti, jump #1, land, take a normal stride, jump #2, land and go forward to jump #3, land and shorten stride to jump #4. Now, after your horse has satisfactorily jumped this exercise, raise #4 in 6-inch increments until your horse can jump 3 feet 6 inches at #4. After one or two repetitions of this entire course, a Preliminary horse should be able to come through the exercise with the obstacles set at 3 feet at #1; 3 feet 6 inches at #2; 2 feet by 5 feet at #3; and 3 feet 6 inches at #4. (However, the first time you do this, I would not be quite that enthusiastic.)

COURSE #7

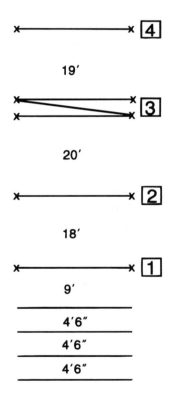

COURSE EIGHT

*C*OURSE Eight is your first introduction to turning over fences in a gymnastic situation. To construct this course, build exercises #1 and #2 first, then measure the distance straight ahead to #5. Put the rails for #5 on the ground so that you can ride through the open standards at #5. Build #3 and #4 so that the left standard of #3 and the right standard of #4 are on the lines formed by #2 to #5. Then angle the rails 45 degrees at #3 and #4 to the line from #2 to #5. Measure the distance from #2 to #3 and from #2 to #4 from the end of the rail at #2 to the end of the rail at #3 and #4. Do not measure from wings, as their widths may vary.

After you trot over the cavalletti, build a jump at #1. Jump this several times, then build the oxer at #2 and jump #1–2 several times. When you are satisfied with your horse's performance, jump #1 to #2 to #3. As you jump #2, open your right rein in the air, bring your left rein against the neck, shift your weight over your right knee as you land, and look at the center of the vertical at #3. You should produce three strides on a mild curve. Jump #1, #2, and #3 several times until the horse understands the turn. Now jump #1, #2, and #4, reversing the aids you used to turn to #3. This exercise should produce two strides on a curve. It will be difficult at first because we have just spent five minutes teaching your horse to jump to the right. Many horses will drift to the right, but once they understand the exercise, they will be come very flexible. After several repetitions in both directions, you will find all you have to do is open one rein over #2 and your horse will seek that curve, to the right or the left, according to your actions.

Give your horse a break now and set the oxer at #5. This should not be too big—3 feet in front and 3 feet 3 inches behind should be sufficient to start. Then trot in, jump #1 and #2, and take four steady strides to #5. The actions of your reins on landing after #2 are the same as the actions you used to handle the short distance between #4 and #5 in Course Six. Land in a light three-point, with your hands at the horse's withers, and squeeze the reins. Do not sit down and pull back or your horse will run through this exercise in three long strides every single time.

COURSE #8

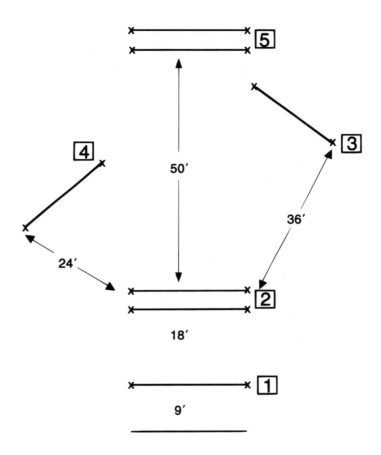

Once you have rehearsed all three lines, you can now start to do a course. For example, trot in, jump #1, #2, #3, and canter #4 backward. Return to the trot, then continue #1, #2, #4, and canter #3 backward. Return to the trot. Trot #1, #2, #5, and halt. And so on, back and forth. If your horse has trouble turning to the left, emphasize that curve; if he has trouble to the right, emphasize that curve. Occasionally, if your horse is extremely excitable, you can jump #1 and #2, halt without jumping #3, #4, or #5, then reassure your horse and walk off. In general, I do not like pulling event horses up in front of obstacles, but I am willing to do it if the horse is extremely difficult.

COURSE #9

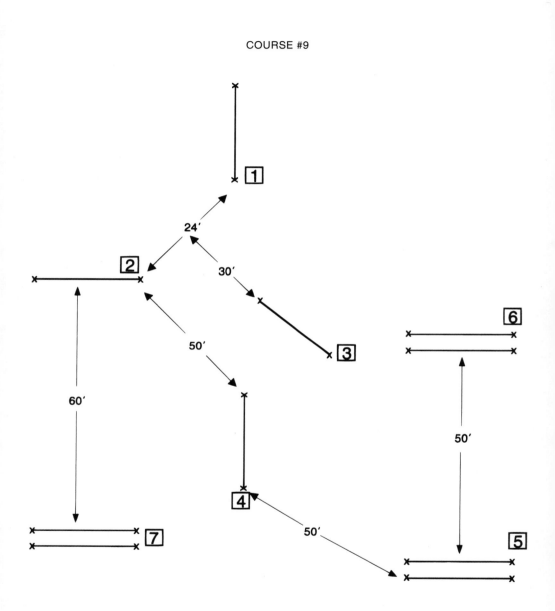

COURSE NINE

$\mathscr{C}$OURSE Nine will improve your horse's ability to jump fences on curves. After warming your horse up, trot and canter back and forth over #1. Then trot and canter your horse back and forth over #2 and then #3. These fences should be set at 2 feet, no more. Then on a circle at a quiet canter, jump #1, #2, #3, and continue—#1, #2, #3, and so on—remaining on the circle for six revolutions. In the air over each obstacle, open your inside rein, put your outside hand against the withers, place your weight over your inside knee, and look at the next jump. The normal horse should produce three strides from #1 to #2, five to six strides from #2 to #3, and five to six strides from #3 to #1. Work in both directions and be sure to note which direction causes your horse more trouble. This is invaluable information for both the cross-country and show jumping phases. After your horse does #1, #2, #3 successfully, canter on the left lead to #3, #1, #2, #4, and #5. This is a bit trickier and calls for a change of direction at #4, rather than just a maintenance of direction at #1, #2, #3.

Return at the canter on the left lead to #5, #4, #2, #1, #3. Once you have the horse turning in both directions, use your imagination. For example, you can go right lead canter #3, #2, #1, #6, then four steady strides to #5. Or, alternatively, you can go left lead canter #3, #1, #2, five steady strides to #7, #5, #4, #2, #1, and so on. Make sure that you develop patterns that work your horse in both directions, with the emphasis on your horse's difficult side. The height of the fences at #1, #2, and #3 can be raised to 3 feet. The fences at #4, #5, and #7 should start at 3 feet but later can be raised to 3 feet six inches.

COURSE #10

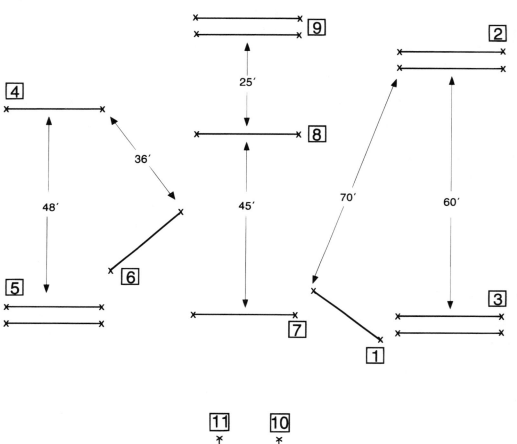

COURSE TEN

$\mathcal{C}$OURSE Ten duplicates various distances that are met on a normal show jumping course. After warming your horse up at the canter over a vertical and an oxer, your first exercise should be to canter from #1 to #2, and later from #2 to #1, on a curved line with six strides. Next, canter on the right lead from #2 to #3 in a steady five strides; and later, on the left lead, from #3 to #2 in four long strides.

Your next exercise should be to canter from #4 to #5 in three normal strides, then again back from #5 to #4. Then approach on a curve from #6 to #4, which you should ride in three curved strides.

After giving your horse a short break, jump #7, #8, #9, which you will ride as three steady strides to one long stride. Advanced horses should also be able to come back from #9 to #8 to #7, one long stride to three short strides. Finally, your horse should rehearse the bounce over #10 and #11 in both directions starting at 2 feet 6 inches. You should gradually raise the bounce rails to 3 feet 6 inches. Work over these exercises in segments rather than trying to jump all eleven obstacles at one time. Set the heights at 3 feet 3 inches to 3 feet 6 inches, especially for your first attempt at handling these distances. Once you are sure you can produce the required number of strides, you can start to raise the height of the obstacles.

COURSE #11

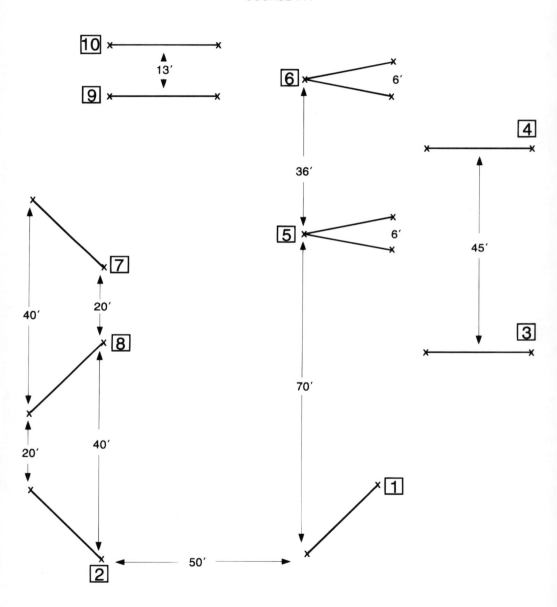

COURSE ELEVEN

OURSE Eleven is a continuation of the work in Course Ten, with a greater emphasis on the accuracy of your approach. Before starting, take all of the rails away from #6 and take the vertical away from #7. Then trot and canter back and forth normally, warming up over #1. Then ride on a curved line from #1 to #2 and from #2 to #1. This should produce quite an attractive five- or six-stride curved line for you. After working in both directions at #1 and #2, canter in both directions over #3 and #4, asking your horse to put three steady strides in each time.

For your next exercise, approach on the right lead and jump from #2 to #8. Aim for the center of the obstacle, jumping #2 at an angle as well as #8 at an angle. Make the line of your approach parallel to the long side of the arena. Practice keeping a straight line in the approach to an angled rail, landing straight, and taking a measured number of strides before taking another fence at an angle.

After you have successfully ridden from #2 to #8, and from #8 to #2, in two steady strides, add the rail at #7. Again, maintain a line that is straight and parallel to the long side while jumping #2, #8, and #7 on angles. Take two strides between each set of rails. Practice on both leads. Once you have done this, come back on the left lead and jump #1 to #5 in a forward five strides. Jump #1 on an angle as you would in the zigzag rail exercises at #2, #8, and #7. As you land over #1, make sure that you keep your eyes fixed on the part of the corner of #5 that you wish to jump. You should be able to go from #1 to #5 and from #5 to #1 equally well. Finally, add the corner at #6, and go in a forward five strides from #1 to #5 and a forward two strides from #5 to #6. Later on, you should come back #6, #5, to #1. Finally, finish with the bounce at #9 to #10 and #10 to #9. All of these obstacles should be set at the height of your level, with the exception of the zigzag rails at #2, #8, and #7, which should be slightly lower at first.

Index

JAMES C. WOFFORD

JIMMY WOFFORD was a mainstay of the U.S. Equestrian Team's three-day event squad for two decades, during which time he was named to four Olympic teams, winning two team silver medals, and five National Championships. In addition, he was the individual silver medalist at the 1980 Alternate Olympics at Fontainebleau, and the individual bronze medalist in the 1970 World Championships at Punchestown.

The son of the USET's first President, Colonel John W. Wofford (himself a 1932 Olympian), Jimmy also has two brothers who have ridden with the USET. After serving a full term as President of the American Horse Shows Association, the national equestrian federation of the United States, Jimmy resumed his activities as one of the country's most sought-after equestrian clinicians and coaches. He has also occupied key roles for the U.S. Combined Training Association, the USET, and the Fédération Équestre Internationale. He lives with his wife and two daughters, all horsewomen, in Upperville, Virginia.